Frantz Fanon

PANAF GREAT LIVES

Other Books in the PGL Series

> *Kwame Nkrumah*
> *Sékou Touré*
> *Nelson Mandela**
> *Eduardo Mondlane*
> *Kanyama Chiume*
> *Sam Nujoma*

*Discontinued

PANAF GREAT LIVES

Frantz Fanon

PANAF

Frantz Fanon

© Copyright Panaf Books 1975
© Copyright Panaf 2001

First Published 1973

All rights reserved. No part of this publication may be reproduced, stored in retrieval system, or transmitted, in any form or by any means, electronic, mechanical, photocopying, recording or otherwise, without the prior permission in writing of Panaf Books, nor be otherwise circulated in any form of binding or cover other than that in which it is published, nor without a similar condition including this condition being imposed on subsequent purchaser.

ISBN 0901787 30 2

Printed and bound in Great Britain by
Antony Rowe Ltd, Eastbourne

PANAF BOOKS

75 Weston Street
London SE1 3RS (UK)

Other Important Panaf Books

Title	Author
Africa Must Unite	*Kwame Nkrumah*
Axioms of Kwame Nkrumah	*Kwame Nkrumah*
Challenge of the Congo	*Kwame Nkrumah*
Class Struggle in Africa	*Kwame Nkrumah*
Consciencism	*Kwame Nkrumah*
Dark Days In Ghana	*Kwame Nkrumah*
I Speak of Freedom	*Kwame Nkrumah*
Neo-Colonialism	*Kwame Nkrumah*
Rhodesia File	*Kwame Nkrumah*
The Struggle Continues	*Kwame Nkrumah*
Forward Ever	June Milne
Kwame Nkrumah — A Biography	June Milne
Kwame Nkrumah: The Conakry Years	June Milne
Where Others Wavered — The Autobiography of Sam Nujoma	Sam Nujoma

CONTENTS

		Page
1	From Martinique	9
2	*Black Skin, White Masks*	19
3	Evolué ideology and the French Left	31
4	Psychiatry and politics	49
5	Fanon and the FLN	59
6	Armed struggle and the All-African People's Conference, Accra 1958	83
7	Fanon and the national bourgeoisie	93
8	Classes and the Algerian Revolution	103
9	Fanon on racism	117
10	The role of women	125
11	To 'put Africa in motion'	133
12	Fanon and the reformist political party	139
13	Problems of leadership	147
14	The battle of the mind	159
	Conclusion	169
	Appendix	178
	Proceedings of the Soumman Conference, 1956. Extracts from the platform.	

ACKNOWLEDGEMENTS

For permission to quote from the following books by Frantz Fanon:

Black Skin, White Masks
   Grove Press Inc., 53 East 11th Street, New York, N.Y. 10003.

A Dying Colonialism
Toward the African Revolution
   Monthly Review Press, 116 West 14th Street, New York, N.Y. 10011.

The Wretched of the Earth
   These extracts are taken from Frantz Fanon's *The Damned* (translated by Constance Farrington) published by *Présence Africaine,* Paris 1963 (and subsequently as *The Wretched of the Earth* by other houses).

ABBREVIATIONS

A L N   National Liberation Army. Formed in 1954.
A M L   Amis du Manifeste de la Liberté. Formed by Ferhat Abbas in 1944.
C C E   Co-ordinating and Executive Council. Set up by the Soumman Conference in 1956.
C N R A   Conseil National de la Révolution. Formed by the Soumann Conference in 1956 to be the supreme authority of the F L N/A L N.
C R U A   Comité Révolutionnaire pour l'Unité et l'Action. Founded in 1954.
F L N   Front de Libération Nationale. Formed in 1954.
G P R A   Provisional Revolutionary Government of Algeria. Formed in 1958.
M T L D   Mouvement pour le Triomphe des Libertés Démocratiques. Founded by Messali Hadj in 1947.
O S   Organization Secrète. Formed in 1947.
P P A   Parti du Peuple Algérien. Founded in 1937.
U D M A   Union Démocratique du Manifesto Algérien.
U G E M A   Union Générale des Etudiants Musulmans Algériens. A branch of the F L N formed in 1955.
U G T A   Union Générale des Travailleurs Algériens. Founded in 1956.
U L E M A   Organization formed by Sheikh Ben Badis in 1931. Nominally a non-political organization to promote Arabic language and culture, i.e. to prevent Algerians from becoming 'assimilated Europeans.'
U N F A   National Union of Algerian women.

I
FROM MARTINIQUE

In France, before 1940, when a West Indian was introduced in Bordeaux or Paris society, the introducer always added, 'from Martinique'.[1]

FRANTZ FANON was born at Fort-de-France, the principal town of Martinique in 1925. At that time the total population of the island was just over a quarter of a million. European contact was established by Columbus, and the Spanish annihilated almost the entire original population of the island. In the era of mercantile capitalism the importance of Martinique was twofold. First, it occupied a strategic position in relation to mainland Africa. Fort-de-France had a fine natural harbour and it is small wonder that in the various wars which broke out in this period between the western powers, Martinique was invariably occupied. The last occupation occurred during the Napoleonic wars when Britain seized the island and restored it to France in 1814. Since then, it has remained a French colony.

On Martinique, the colonizers saw a country ideally suited for the establishment of plantations which would produce much needed raw materials such as sugar, coffee and vanilla. Since the indigenous population had been exterminated it became necessary to import slaves and this was done on a large scale in the early eighteenth century. Fanon's ancestors thus came from Africa and he himself was the grandson of a slave.

When slavery was abolished on the island, slave mentality still persisted. France has boasted that in its relationship with its colonial subjects, there was no question of colour discrimination. This deception worked for a while, for compared to the British, the French system involved the creation of a class known as the evolué, members of which had opportunities and certain legal rights. While the British relied on tribalism and religion to implement the policy of divide and rule, the sophisticated French added a further division in the creation of the evolués.

In Martinique, the division was along class lines. Out of the colonized, who were both oppressed and exploited, the

French created a class of evolués to which it granted the political, economic and social privileges accorded to its own middle class. At the time of Fanon's birth, France had established local municipal councils based on adult suffrage and the people could elect a senator and two deputies to the French Assembly in Paris. On the other hand, no colonial found his way into the British House of Commons. A Martiniquan could boast then that theoretically he could become a member of the French Assembly. Fanon wrote that before 1939, the West Indian claimed to be happy, or at least thought of himself as being so. He voted, went to school when he could, took part in processions, drank rum and danced the beguine. 'Those who were privileged to go to France spoke of Paris . . . And those who were not privileged to know Paris let themselves be beguiled.'[2]

Before the Second World War, the conscious section of the Martiniquans saw exploitation which cut across colour lines. They saw no national oppression. Fanon wrote that in Martinique it was rare to find hardened racial positions, since the racial problem was covered over by economic discrimination. Relations were not modified by epidermal accentuations. 'Despite the greater or lesser amount of melanin that the skin may contain, there is a tacit agreement enabling all and sundry to recognize one another as doctors, tradesmen, workers. A Negro worker will be on the side of the mulatto worker against the middle-class Negro. Here we have proof that questions of race are but a superstructure, a mantle, an obscure ideological emanation concealing an economic reality.'[3] For the evolué in Martinique the sky was the limit, and he saw the same opportunities being offered for personal advancement by the French system as for members of its own petty bourgeoisie. The evolués' aspirations became those of the entire people, and it was they who transmitted the idea to the people that they were French, and not a colonized people.

In 1939, on the eve of the Second World War, the social pyramid in Martinique consisted of the following classes: at the apex were the French, consisting of the plantation owners, top civil servants and the big traders; this small section which had economic power also possessed political power. At the base was the mass of the workers, both urban and rural. In between, were the evolués, a tiny group drawn from the Martiniquans. The evolués were distinguishable from the rest of the people in that they had formal education and owned a small amount of property.

If there was one single event which accelerated the growth of the national movements in Asia and Africa it was the Second World War. In their embryonic stages in the 1930s, the national movements were given a fillip as a result of the war. The colonial oppressed were drawn in to it because it was a war between the older imperialist powers and the rising fascist countries represented by Nazi Germany. To win the minds of the oppressed, the colonialists said that the war was being fought against fascist dictatorships and racism, as exemplified by Nazism. It was fought for the preservation of democracy, freedom and equality. It was only after the war that the oppressed peoples realized that these slogans of freedom did not apply to them.

Before the war, Martinique was not affected by the convulsions which were beginning to rip capitalist society apart, and the strong currents of the national movements had still to touch its shores. But the global conflict which broke out also shook Martinique as it did almost every colony. First, France was overrun by the Germans and occupied. In Vietnam, the colonial people had risen against France and were on the point of winning their freedom. The war was in reality a conflict between those capitalist powers which had colonies and those which had not. But it had the effect of awakening the minds of the oppressed. Events blew sky high the myth that the colonial masters were mighty and invincible. Oppressed peoples realized that they too could win their freedom and independence. It was thinking along such lines which had the effect of liberating them from their slave mentality.

Martinique was affected in a concrete and practical way, although it was spared the ravages of war. The capitulation of the French government and the installation of a puppet pro-Nazi regime in Paris set in motion a train of events on the island which Fanon describes. 'The downfall of France, for the West Indian, was in a sense the murder of a father. This national defeat might have been endured as it was in the metropolis, but a good part of the French fleet remained blockaded in the West Indies during the four years of the German occupation,'[4] and Fort-de-France was "invaded" by nearly ten thousand Europeans.

These Pétainist sailors and soldiers did not engage in production and had to be fed from the surplus which the people produced. The West Indian economy suffered a severe blow, for it became necessary to find, at a time when nothing could be imported, the wherewithal to feed 10,000 men. To add to the difficulties, many sailors and soldiers sent for their wives and children, who had to be housed and fed. Before then, there were about 2,000 French people in Martinique, and they had well-defined functions in the economy and body politic of the island. These, according to Fanon, had integrated into the social life of the colony, and did not show any outward manifestations of racialism, though they kept the masses at a distance.

It was different with the European sailors and soldiers. They were drawn from the workers and peasants but centuries of oppression had poisoned their minds and they had become chauvinistic. Like the poor whites of South Africa and America, they regarded themselves as superior to the colonial subjects although they were exploited just as ruthlessly as France's black subjects. These men, lacking the sophistication of the upper classes, could not conceal their racialism. The Martiniqans felt the full impact of racial arrogance and racial prejudice. Fanon analysing this, wrote: 'The four years during which they were obliged to live shut in on themselves, inactive, a prey to anguish when they thought of their families left in France, victims of despair as to the future, allowed them to drop a mask which, when all is said and done, was rather superficial, and to behave as "authentic racists".'[5]

The soldiers and sailors did not do any productive work, for they were not trained to do anything but to fight. The people now in their contact with these drones saw their real relationship with France. As producers, the people of Martinique were supporting not only the 2,000 French residents but also these thousands of soldiers and sailors. For this labour, they received no thanks but increased arrogance and prejudice. They were despised and insulted by the very men whom they carried on their backs and shoulders.

Racialism did not see class, and its whiplash affected every section of the Martiniquan population. The result was that the racialism of the soldiers had the effect of forging unity between the evolués and urban and rural workers. Fanon has described graphically the beginnings of resistance, when for example, West Indians began refusing to take off their hats while the 'Marseillaise' was being played. But resistance did not lead to the national struggle for independence, let alone revolution despite the magnificent display of non-collaboration by the people. Lack of political consciousness and lack of organization prevented the people of Martinique from forming a united front against their oppressors and exploiters. They did not see the 2,000 French residents and the soldiers and sailors as different arms of the same body. Rather they saw the fight as one essentially between the French and the Germans, and they categorized the 10,000 soldiers and sailors as 'Germans'. The struggle thus was against the 'Germans', and it was against them that they rose in revolt. Fanon wrote of this final phase of the people's resistance and showed how in 1943, weary of an ostracism to which they were not accustomed, the West Indians, who had formerly been separated into closed sociological groups, formed a common front against the enemy. Supported by the local army, they fought for and won the rallying of the colony to the Free French. This led to massive demonstrations at which the West Indians celebrated their victory; and according to Fanon the months of July and August 1943 saw the birth of the proletariat.

The lack of clarity at this stage of the national movement showed in the fact that the people were not able to see that the Free French of De Gaulle and the collaborators, whom they labelled 'German', represented the same

French imperialism which stood for their oppression and exploitation. That is why the resistance which really began in 1939, and which in the end led to an armed uprising, did not lead to the overthrow of French imperialism. Rather it led to its entrenchment. The reason for this was the leadership of the struggle was in the hands of the evolués and certain sections of the French Left. The French could well be satisfied with all their investment in creating a class of evolués. At a time of crisis, when they were at their weakest, it was the evolués who came to their rescue and who guided the resistance along channels which would safeguard the French Empire.

In April 1943 Fanon joined the Free French Movement in Dominica and returned to Martinique with the units which liberated it. Having finished his schooling, and with this short period of military experience behind him, Fanon joined the Free French in 1944 and went to Europe. He saw action in Morocco, Algeria and France. Little is known of this time in his life. Fanon himself was reticent about these experiences. But it is likely that Fanon began to perceive the way in which the West Indians had been duped by the French led by De Gaulle into fighting for traditional French interests in the guise of some supposedly common struggle for freedom.

Fanon refers in *Black Skin, White Masks* to his surprise at finding similarly unpleasant racial tensions and attitudes in North Africa and France to those which had arisen in Martinique following its occupation by the forces of Marshal Pétain. However, the processes of disillusionment do not appear to have prevented Fanon from being regarded by his French officers as an excellent soldier. Having been wounded in action in 1945, Fanon was awarded the Croix de Guerre by Colonel Salan, then leading the Sixth Regiment of the 'Tirailleurs Sénégalais'. Ironically, Salan later became one of the major figures to fight against the liberation of Algeria.

After the war, Fanon returned to Martinique with the rank of corporal, and in 1946 he and his brother helped in the election campaign of Aimé Césaire, the principal leader of the evolués. Césaire had been a teacher at the private lycée which Fanon attended in Fort-de-France, and had made a deep impression on him with his message that black was beautiful, and that blacks should be proud of their blackness. This had caught the imagination of the rising generation of educated youth in Martinique. In Fanon, then only sixteen years old, Césaire had found an ardent disciple. For the first time, a lycée teacher, and man therefore who was apparently worthy of respect, was heard to announce quite simply to West Indian society 'that it is fine and good to be a negro'.[6]

At that time Fanon did not realize that while Césaire was with them, chanting and dancing that 'it is good to be a negro', he was in fact leading them to Paris. It was only in 1958 that the role of this leader was thoroughly exposed, certainly to Fanon. The occasion was when France gave its colonies three alternatives. There could be total independence, or total integration, or independence within the French Community. Guinea took the road of total independence, even if it meant poverty. Most of the African colonies took the third alternative of independence within the Community. But Martinique voted for total integration. This was due to the efforts of people like Césaire.

The people also saw through Césaire when they rose in revolt in 1959. This revolt lasted for only three days, but in this short time they were able to hold the capital, Fort-de-France, for a few hours. The Césaires now had to rely on France to come to their rescue to defend and protect them from their own people. The man they had sent to Paris as their deputy in 1945, they now turned against. This was a landmark in the increasing political consciousness of the people of Martinique.

Even although the struggle in Martinique was frustrated, a section of the evolués realized that it could never be the same again. Post-war France was weak and divided and not the pillar of stability and strength. France as a major power was gone for good, and this they saw. Not only was it crushed by the Germans, and defeated by the Japanese, but what was more to the point, a colonial people like themselves, the Vietnamese, had risen in revolt and had defeated the French.

Meanwhile, a few had become aware of a new force that was emerging. This was the continent of Africa where the people were expressing their aspirations through their national liberation movements. What these movements stood for apart from demanding political freedom was not clear. But the intellectuals of the West Indies were drawn to Africa as if pulled by a powerful magnet. Fanon described the gravitational pull of Africa, and its impact on his fellow intellectuals. 'Thus the West Indian, after 1945, changed his values. Whereas before 1939 he had his eyes riveted on white Europe, whereas what seemed good to him was escape from his colour, in 1945 he discovered himself to be not only black but a Negro, and it was in the direction of distant Africa that he was henceforth to put out his feelers. The West Indian in France was continually recalling that he was not a Negro: from 1945 on, the West Indian in France was continually to recall that he *was* a negro.'[7]

Hitherto, West Indians made pretensions of superiority over Africans, but now they came to Africa as penitents. Fanon showed the change. He described the West Indians who came to Africa after 1945 as appearing with 'their hands stretched out, their backs bowed, humbly suppliant. They came to Africa with their hearts full of hope, eager to rediscover the source, to suckle at the authentic breasts of the African earth. The West Indians, civil servants and military, lawyers and doctors, landing in Dakar, were distressed at not being sufficiently black. Fifteen years before, they said to the Europeans, "Don't pay attention to my black skin, it's the sun that has burned me, my soul is as white as yours". After 1945 they changed their tune. They said to the Africans, "Don't pay attention to my white skin, my soul is as black as yours, and that is what matters".'[8]

This objective record of the qualitative change produced by the war on the thinking of the evolués first appeared in *Esprit*, a French review, in 1955. It was written two years after the publication of Fanon's first book *Black Skin, White Masks*. The metamorphosis in the thinking of the evolués is seen in retrospect. Fanon like any talented and intelligent youth, who by the end of the war was barely twenty, was seized by the desire to win fame and glory, and wanted to go down in history as a great man like his idol Aimé Césaire. He too, like other evolués, decided to storm Paris. In 1947, he left Martinique to study medicine in France.

2

BLACK SKIN, WHITE MASKS

Every time a man has contributed to the victory of the dignity of the spirit, every time a man has said no to an attempt to subjugate his fellows, I have felt solidarity with his act.[1]

FANON was able to gain entrance to Lyon University in France, to study medicine and psychiatry. Universities in the post-war period reflected society in turmoil. They had become hotbeds of radical and revolutionary ideas. France had suffered humiliating defeats at the hands of the Germans, the Japanese and the Vietnamese. To many, France had now become a decadent nation, and something radical had to be done to infuse it with new vigour and life, for there could be no return to the past. Classes again contended for supremacy and the universities became cockpits for contending ideas.

It was not possible for a sensitive and intelligent youth like Fanon to stand aloof. A person of his temperament would have been involved in any case in some radical cause. But in addition he could not get away from the fact impressed on him daily that he belonged to a people who were oppressed and who were being treated as second-class citizens in France. He founded and became the editor of a student magazine named *Tom Tom*. It was controlled by black students and was directed chiefly at them. It was not long before he attracted the attention of evolués from Africa and the West Indies associated with the magazine *Présence Africaine*. It was through this magazine that he was able to meet and to form a close association with the current celebrity of Western intellectuals, Jean-Paul Sartre. This association and friendship he retained for the rest of his short life.

It has been a tradition in French society that an intellectual, if he is to become famous, must write a book. It could be a play, a novel, a political or philosophical treatise. It could also be a hard-hitting criticism of an existing book, for nothing added spice to the otherwise drabness and dullness of middle class life than something new and controversial. A book meant that society would open its doors to the writer and he would enter the sanctuary of the elect.

Fanon's first book, *Black Skin, White Masks* was published in 1952, when he had finished his medical studies. It dealt with a hitherto unexplored subject of the white-black relationship, from the point of view and from the voice of the black man. Fanon saw it as a clinical study, for 'the juxtaposition of the white and black races has created a massive psycho-existential complex'.[2] He hoped that by analysing it, he would destroy this mental disease.

The method of analysis he followed was the same that he had been taught in medical school. First, there was to be observation to detect the symptoms, and then he would proceed to diagnosis. The remedy would flow from this diagnosis. Commenting on this new and developing social and political question, the crisis of colour, he says, 'Since I was born in the Antilles, my observations and my conclusions are valid only for the Antilles – at least concerning the black man *at home*'.[3] He wanted to know why it was that black men wore white masks; and the processes and the mentality which made them seek 'whiteness'. But the black man he spoke about was not the worker or the peasant, but the evolué. It was to him, and to the radical section of the French intellectuals, that he addressed himself. In a capitalist society, particularly in its earlier stages, there were always openings for any one from the lower class with drive, initiative and talent to climb up and become part of the upper class. The evolués were trying to do something different. They sought through education and a process of acculturation to become assimilated into French society. But they forgot, and were reminded, that they belonged to an oppressed group whose parents were slaves.

The evolués, despite French talk of equality and assimilation were in reality shut out, and except for a few were even denied the ordinary courtesy given to fellow human beings. Fanon however deals with a period when the evolués looked at colour discrimination as an individual problem. The evolués just wanted to move out of the milieu that stunted their growth and into where they would be given opportunity to develop their talents to the fullest capacity. In talking about the negro, Fanon is really dealing with the evolué, of his ambitions, his dreams, his schemes and plans to escape the grim realities of oppression and exploitation which was the lot of the people in the colonies.

The evolué carried with him the deadly disease of slave mentality, manifesting itself in an inferiority complex. The evolué did not believe in the strength and power of his people in Martinique. He did not believe that by collective action he could get rid of all his own basic problems as well as that of the people. He rather accepted the values, mores and ideologies of the oppressors and he strove to find himself a niche in the arena where power resided. In doing so he separated himself from the people.

One way that Fanon observes the evolué did so was by abandoning Creole, spoken by the people, and learning to master the French language, the language of the dominant class. He observed that middle class people in the Antilles only spoke Creole to their servants. The schoolchildren of Martinique were taught to scorn the dialect. Some families completely forbade the use of Creole and mothers ridiculed their children for speaking it. Thus the two institutions of society, namely the school and family evolved to inculcate ideas in the young, were orientated towards France and Paris as far as the middle class families in the Antilles were concerned. Fanon said that one of the deadliest insults that one could deliver to an evolué was to say that 'He doesn't even know how to speak French'.[4] The mastery of the French language had this consequence: 'The Antilles Negro who wants to be white will be the whiter as he gains greater mastery of the cultural tool that language is.'[5] But he also shows another angle for: 'the Negro wants to speak French because it is the key that can open doors which were still barred to him fifty years ago. In the Antilles Negro who comes within this study we find a quest for subtleties, for refinements of language – so many further means of proving to himself that he has measured up to the culture.'[6] He relates two anecdotes from his own personal experience on this score. In the election campaign of 1945, Aimé Césaire, who was seeking a seat as a deputy to the French Assembly, addressed a large audience at a boys' school. In the middle of his speech a woman fainted. The next day an acquaintance told him about this and commented that she had fainted because his French refinement of style was so exciting. The second involved himself personally while at Lyon. In a lecture he had compared Negro and European poetry, and a French acquaintance had told him enthusiastically: 'At bottom you are a white man'[7]. Fanon added rather bitterly, 'the fact that I had been able to investigate so interesting a problem through the white man's language gave me honorary citizenship'.[8] Fanon resented such praise. It smacked of condescension and patronage, both of which revealed a deep-seated racism.

In France, the evolué encountered racial prejudice everywhere. It was the language which conveyed this. The manner in which Frenchmen spoke to the blacks whether the Frenchman was a doctor, teacher, priest or policeman showed that he did not accept the evolué as an equal. Thus while the evolué spoke French perfectly he would be addressed by the Frenchman in 'pidgin nigger'. Fanon gives an example of how a Catholic priest addressed the only black student in a group: 'You go 'way big Savannah, what for and come 'long us?'[9] The reply in perfect French unsettled the priest, and caused laughter. But this was what every evolué experienced some time or other in his contact with the whites. Fanon concludes that 'a white man addressing a Negro behaves exactly like an adult with a child'.[10]

A society riddled with racialism is sick. But this sickness affects both the colonizer and the colonized. At a certain stage, as a reaction to white racialism, black racialism raises its head. Thus the very people who complain of French racialism show racialism towards others. If the evolués complained of the French trying to place obstacles in the way of their advancement, the evolués in their turn resented others from climbing up to their position.

Amongst the colonized people the French created a hierarchy. Those from Martinique occupied a higher rung in the ladder than those from Africa, for instance. This showed itself in the preferential treatment meted out to certain members of the oppressed peoples in the allocation of jobs. Those from the Antilles were absorbed into French army units while those from Africa were placed in special apartheid platoons and battalions. It was this distinction that made the evolués believe that they were French and had nothing in common with their colonial counterparts.

Fanon records this racial prejudice amongst the oppressed themselves when he wrote that he had known people born in Dahomey or the Congo who pretended to be natives of the Antilles, and Antilles Negroes who were annoyed at being thought Senegalese. 'This is because the Antilles Negro is more "civilized" than the African, that is, he is closer to the white man; and this difference prevails not only in back streets and on boulevards but also in public service and the army'.[11]

He traces racialism amongst the oppressed as being the direct result of the policy of indoctrination by the ruling class: 'The Frenchman does not like the Jew, who does not like the Arab, who does not like the Negro . . . The Arab is told: "If you are poor, it is because the Jew has bled you and taken everything from you." The Jew is told: "You are not of the same class as the Arab because you are really white and because you have Einstein and Bergson." The Negro is told: "You are the best soldiers in the French Empire; the Arabs think they are better than you, but they are wrong." '[12]

Fanon had his own personal experiences to relate on this score. He was stopped many times in broad daylight by policemen who mistook him for an Arab; and when they discovered his origins, they were obsequious in their apologies, saying that of course they knew that a Martiniquan was quite different from an Arab. 'I always protested violently, but I was always told, "You don't know them".'[13]

It was because of this division amongst the oppressed that it was possible for the rulers to use troops from one colony to suppress national movements in other colonies. Units of African troops, for example, were sent to Vietnam. Fanon noted that whenever there has been any attempt at insurrection, the military authorities usually ordered only coloured soldiers into action. 'They were "men of colour" who nullified the liberation efforts of other "men of colour".'[14]

Fanon saw the sickness of racialism in the French, in the Martiniquans, Jews, and Senegalese. The whole of Europe, he declared, had a racist structure. France was a racist country for the myth of the 'bad nigger' was part of the 'collective unconscious'. From childhood, not only the French, but the colonized people themselves, were indoctrinated with the myth that black was a symbol of evil. The torturer was a black man; Satan was black; and when one was dirty one was black. This applied to both physical and moral dirt. Fanon remarked that it would be astonishing, if trouble were taken to bring them all together, to see the vast number of expressions implying that the black man personified sin.

The ruling class marshalled a battery of experts from scholarly anthropologists to world renowned anatomists to prove that the skulls of the black races were inferior. Either they had smaller craniums than the whites or their mental makeup was such as to grope towards someone who was stronger than themselves. One such expert was Professor O. Mannoni who wrote the book *Prospero and Caliban: Psychology of Colonization*. This racist author based his sweeping generalizations on the study of the history, politics and psychology of the Malagasy people. Rationalizing the conquest by French imperialism the author asserted that the Malagasy people had a dependency complex and that is why they accepted the new masters without resistance. Fanon singled out the views of this author for attack.

The polemic against Mannoni is not important now, because since the granting of political independence to the colonies open racism as propounded by Mannoni has been discarded. However, Fanon also turned his pen against fellow evolués because they were running away from the fight. He knew that every evolué on landing in France felt the blast of racism. The evolué was confronted with two alternatives, either to stand with the white world and incline towards a certain degree of universality, or to reject Europe and to cling to the company of his fellow evolués. If the latter, the ghetto existence would tend to make the evolué attempt to portray an idyllic life in Africa before the slave trade and colonization. Fanon cites the example of Alioune Diop, of Présence Africaine, who wrote *La Philosophie bantoue*. In it Diop says: 'The double question that arises is to determine whether the genius of the black man should cultivate what constitutes his individuality, that youth of spirit, that innate respect for man and creation, that joy of living . . . One wonders too what the Negro can contribute to the modern world . . . What we can say is that the very idea of culture conceived as a revolutionary will is as contrary to our genius as the very idea of progress. Progress would have haunted our consciousness only if we had grievances against life, which is a gift of nature'.[15]

Not only was Diop's vision of an ideal society to which Africa could contribute, utopian, but it was also reactionary and dangerous. The reality in South Africa was segregation, and when 75,000 African miners went out on strike in 1946, the state police forced them back to work with rifles and bayonets. This to Fanon was the grim reality of apartheid which banished the Negro from participating in modern history as a free and independent force. Fanon dismissed Diop's fantasy with: 'There is nothing ontological about segregation. Enough of this rubbish'.[16] With such a standpoint it did not take long for the youthful and fiery Fanon to challenge the bogus philosophy of negritude.

Fanon recognized that racialism with its superiority and inferority complexes was created by men to perpetuate a particular social structure. Having diagnosed the illness, he proposed a cure. We must abandon hallucinatory attempts of whitening, but act to change the social structure. He was, however, not clear in *Black Skin, White Masks* about how this should be done.

Black Skin, White Masks is important because it throws light on what was agitating Fanon in the formative period of his life, at a time when French society had become a seething cauldron of contradictory and antagonistic ideas. It shows him to be a serious thinker who was prepared to get to grips with the problems of the age which were regarded as important to his fellow evolués. Official French society allows its youth to be rebels, and in this book, Fanon the youth, is seen as a rebel, rebelling against the system that was condemning the black man to be nothing more than a hewer of wood and a drawer of water. Fanon used all the intellectual strength at his command to expose the apologists of racialism. But in doing so, he also had to fight dangerous ideas from his own fellow evolués who were succumbing to myths and mysticism. He saw their excessive preoccupation over problems of culture was just a form of escapism. In the struggle against the former, it was not enough to master the French language, but it was also necessary to absorb the vast storehouse of ideas which is a legacy of mankind, and which the bourgeoisie offers to a few of its intellectuals. There is little doubt that when Fanon was a student he read voraciously till his eyes pained. But this was necessary if one was to fight back at the ideologists of the bourgeoisie.

It was remarkable that one who was barely 25 years of age could speak and write so knowledgeably on such a variety of subjects. Being a psychiatrist, it was not surprising that he frequently mentions Adler, Freud and Jung in his books. He knew the writings of Rousseau, Voltaire and Montesquieu. It is obvious too that he had more than scanned the works of classical French novelists like Balzac and Zola. His reference to Alan Paton showed that he was also concerned with what was happening in South Africa, and that he was well versed in the English language. He mentions the modern writers fashionable in that period but who have passed away into obscurity. He however made a special study of the racial question, and was equipped to tackle the racist Mannoni. Last but not least, he read the latest on politics, for he was passionately interested in the oppressed people and the national liberation movements, particularly in South Africa, the Malagasy Republic and in Indo-China.

In his polemics he used all that language could offer to demolish the arguments of his opponents. He used sarcasm, irony, innuendo to hit at his opponents. In this he scored points and pushed them on the defensive. Yet his strongest point both against French racists and his fellow evolués was to show *reality*. The strongest argument against Mannoni's false theory of dependency complex, was that the people of the Malagasy Republic rose in revolt against their French oppressors and were only crushed after one of the most savage repressions known in Africa, paralleled only by that of the British against the agrarian movement of the Kenyan people in the fifties, known as the Mau-Mau.

Later upsurges of the Malagasy people show Fanon right and the racist Mannoni wrong. Likewise, the Indo-Chinese have continued their struggle for almost three generations for freedom and independence, and not because they have discovered a culture of their own.

The logic of his polemics led him to a position where he recognized the national liberation movements in areas like Indo-China to be the new reality of the age. He saw that only a successful struggle for national liberation could begin to solve the problem of racism. The two were interconnected with one depending on the other. In this book however, he had not fully worked out the problem. It was only a few years later when the Algerian Revolution broke out that his views crystallized. In *Black Skin, White Masks,* he had attempted merely to interpret the world. His participation in the Algerian Revolution showed that he was then setting about to change it.

In this early book the reader sees Fanon's wit and flashes of brilliance, but above all the reader is struck by his honesty. Fanon was fearless both in his thinking as well as in his personal life. The French rulers who regarded the giving of education to evolués as a favour, did not take lightly some of them studying scientific socialism with passion and interest. Marx was taboo. If he had to be mentioned then he had to be attacked. Fanon relates how the rulers dropped their masks when someone spoke of communism. 'When a Negro talks of Marx, the first reaction is always the same: "We have brought you up to our level and now you turn against your benefactors. Ingrates! Obviously nothing can be expected of you".[17]

Amongst the intellectuals of the oppressed there is a thin line at times that divides the rebel from a revolutionary. In *Black Skin, White Masks* Fanon is a rebel. Four years later, the Algerian struggle for national independence and liberation was to turn him into a revolutionary.

3
FANON: EVOLUÉ IDEOLOGY AND THE FRENCH LEFT

To fight for national culture means in the first place to fight for the liberation of the nation, that material keystone which makes the building of a culture possible. There is no other fight for culture which can develop apart from the popular struggle.[1]

DURING the years between Fanon's joining of the French army, in 1944, and the taking up of his appointment as Head of the Psychiatric Department of the Blida-Joinville Hospital in Algeria in 1953, Fanon became deeply involved in the ideological cross currents of evolués and the French intelligentsia. This was the time of the growth of the concepts of negritude and existentialism amongst evolués and radicalized intellectuals.

The Second World War left France weak and exhausted, and the French bourgeoisie disgraced and discredited. It had become very vulnerable because sections had capitulated to the Nazis, while it was the workers, peasants and intellectuals who had provided the backbone of the resistance. Guns were therefore in the hands of the resistance movement after liberation. The Communist Party of France emerged with tremendous prestige, for the maquis, the French guerrillas, were led in many instances by members of the party who had distinguished themselves by their heroism and ardour for the cause. With such popularity and backed by people, many of whom were armed, the party was in a better position to tackle the bourgeoisie. But the leadership hesitated. The bourgeoisie had thrown it a concession in the form of a few seats in the cabinet in a coalition government and thus was able to avert a potentially revolutionary situation.

While the French bourgeoisie adopted a policy of co-existence which it knew to be temporary, it gave battle on the ideological field. Two mortal enemies of capitalism and imperialism are its own working class and the oppressed colonial peoples. The danger to the bourgeoisie lay in the ideological field where a section of the intellectuals cast their lot with the workers and with the colonial peoples. This could create an explosive situation which it might not be able to handle. With their education, with their technical know-how, and the vast arena of knowledge which capitalism puts at their disposal, the intellectuals could pose a real danger if these were put at the service of the workers and the oppressed colonial peoples.

The bourgeoisie knew from its own experience that although its grave digger was the proletariat, those who provided it with knowledge and ideology came from a section of the bourgeoisie itself. In fact, developing capitalism cannot help but hurl section after section from its own class into the ranks of the workers. Driving a wedge between ideologists of the colonial peoples and its own radicalized intellectuals, there developed the growth of negritude and existentialism which for a time threatened to check the advance of scientific socialism.

The advocates of negritude were grouped around the journal *Présence Africaine,* and one of their leaders was Fanon's early idol, Aimé Césaire. The journal was founded in 1947 by the Senegalese writer, Alioune Diop. It was to be a mainly cultural periodical, and among its more notable supporters were Gide, Mounier, Senghor and Paul Hazoumé. Writing in the first issue, Alioune Diop declared:

> This review does not fall within the range of any political or philosophical ideology. It seeks the collaboration of all men of good will (white, yellow or black) who are capable of helping us to define the nature of the African essence, and hastening its integration into the modern world.

In opposition to 'white culture' the advocates of negritude sought to revive the culture of Africa. They idealized the past with all its myths and superstitions. Sartre considered negritude as a means to an end, and not an end in itself. The end is a society free from racist consciousness. Negritude, therefore, while a powerful cultural expression must not be confused with a political movement. The goal of negritude was to rise above it and to make it unnecessary.

But according to Senghor, the African is 'a field of pure sensation'; he does not measure or observe, but 'lives' a situation; and this way of acquiring 'knowledge' by confrontation and intuition is 'Negro African'. Kwame

Nkrumah in his essay on African socialism has exposed the ideology of negritude as a 'characteristic' expression of African bourgeois mentality. 'This pseudo-intellectual theory serves as a bridge between the African foreign-dominated middle class and the French cultural establishment. It is irrational, racist and non-revolutionary'.[2]

Fanon was initially drawn to the idea of negritude, and called on intellectuals to turn to Césaire for inspiration and guidance. But later he saw the limitations and dangers of such a concept, and rejected it. In the concluding chapter of *Black Skin, White Masks*, he stated his position very clearly when he quoted Marx: 'The social revolution . . . cannot draw its poetry from the past, but only from the future. It cannot begin with itself before it has stripped itself of all its superstitions concerning the past. Earlier revolutions relied on memories out of world history in order to drug themselves against their own content. In order to find their own content, the revolutions of the nineteenth century have to let the dead bury the dead. Before, the expression exceeded the content; now the content exceeds the expression'.[3]

Marx and Engels had spoken of the alienation of the workers in a capitalist society from an analysis of the capitalist mode of production when the social product was appropriated by the capitalist. Fanon saw similar alienation amongst the masses of the oppressed. Just as Marx had said that the only way to solve the contradiction between capital and the workers was by the latter expropriating the former, so too Fanon said that no appeal to reason or respect of human dignity could alter reality. For the negro plantation worker there was only one solution – to fight.

Fanon recognized that there was also the intellectual alienation of the evolué from a dominant class which was racist. For racist society had driven the evolué into a corner ideologically. He was told that black people had no history, no civilization, no philosophy. Biologically they were so constituted that they lacked refinement, and higher intelligence, and their bodily structures were capable of generating only emotion. When the evolués came out with black racism the rulers were happy, because with such ideas the evolués would never be able to mobilize the masses. This became very apparent when the political leadership from among the advocates of negritude and black racism soon became the most ardent supporters of the status quo. For example, Senghor, President of Senegal and a strong advocate of negritude as well as of the bogus concept of 'African socialism', is among the most backward looking rulers of contemporary Africa.

Fanon saw that the followers of negritude in facing the past had turned their backs on their fellow workers and peasants. He spoke at both the Congresses of Negro Writers and Artists. At the first Congress, held in Paris in September 1956, his theme was 'Racism and Culture'. Three years later, at the Second Congress, held in Rome in 1959, when Fanon was fully involved in the Algerian Revolution, he chose his theme as 'The Reciprocal Basis of National Cultures and Struggles for Liberation'. By pointing to the struggles for liberation he was in fact suggesting to his fellow evolués that they turn their faces to their fellow workers and peasants.

In his opening address in 1959 he said: 'On the occasion of the last Congress, devoted to the crisis of Negro-African culture, the cultural phenomenon was analysed in its relationship with colonial domination. It was said then that racism bloated and disguised the face of a culture that practised it. Racism was seen in literature, wit, songs for schoolgirls, proverbs, habits and patterns. On the other hand it was noted that when a people had undertaken the struggle for liberation they rarely legitimized race prejudice. Even in the course of acute periods of insurrectional armed struggle, one never witnessed the recourse to biological justification.' To him at the second Congress, the fundamental problems of Negro-African culture, unity and interdependence of culture in its renaissance, boiled down to a specific problem, whether 'we shall liberate ourselves without aftermath from an alienation which for centuries has made us the great absentees from history'.

Whereas in the first Congress he spoke as one evolué to

another, in the second, it was as an evolué who had enmeshed himself in the Algerian struggle for liberation. In the first he was the rebel evolué. In the second he had become a revolutionary intellectual, and he spoke as one. Whereas in the first congress he was treading on ground with which the evolués were familiar, in the second he was treading on new ground not familiar to the evolués, that of liberation. He recalled in his second address how the rulers, in order to destroy the manhood of the oppressed, attempted to destroy their culture. While the mass of the people resisted, a section went over and tried to acquire the culture of the oppressor. He noted that the culture of the oppressed under colonization was an arrested culture with a stock of habits and outworn traditions. He pointed out that the poverty of the people, national oppression and arrested culture were part of the same thing. He said that after a century of colonial domination, one found a culture which had become rigid in its existence, sedimentary and fossilized.

With the struggle for liberation a change took place. Previously, the evolué wrote facing the oppressor and colonizer, either to charm or to denounce him; now he addressed himself to the people. He gave a concrete instance of a storyteller in Algeria who after 1952 or 1953 completely overhauled both the method of exposition as well as the content of his recitals. The impact of the liberation struggle was such that every time a storyteller recounts a new episode to his audience, it was possible to discern the existence of a new type of man. The storyteller restored liberty to his imagination, innovated and performed works of originality. The effect on the intellectual was that his writing lost the character of despair, for he identified with the people, and his struggle became a part of their struggle.

Fanon, at the Second Congress, posed sharply the question of the relationship between struggle, whether political or armed, and culture. His answer to it was clear and unequivocal: 'We think that organized and conscious struggle taken by the colonized people to restore the sovereignty of the nation constitutes the most fully cultural manifestation there is'. He added, however, that 'the struggle for liberation does not give national culture back its old values and contours; this struggle which aims at a fundamental redistribution between men cannot leave either the cultural form or the content of these people intact. After the struggle there is not only the disappearance of colonialism, but also the disappearance of the colonized.' Attacking those who scoffed at nationalism and labelled it reactionary he said : 'Far from separating itself from other nations, it is national liberation which brings the nation on to the stage of history'.

Fanon's conception of culture, although he maintained that the highest form of cultural manifestation of an oppressed people is through the struggle for liberation, was nevertheless limited. In this, he was in line with the intellectuals attached to the bourgeoisie who dominated the Second Congress of Negro Writers and Artists, and who believed that what the workers create and produce cannot be regarded as culture.

The ideological struggle between the proletariat and the bourgeoisie uses two different and diametrically opposite views on culture. Culture, according to the proletariat, includes all material and spiritual values as well as the activities of man in society. It regards material achievements like the invention of machinery, tools, and experiences in the conquest of nature, as much a part of culture as, for example, achievements in art, literature, philosophy, ethics, education and sculpture. Although spiritual and cultural changes do not automatically bring about material changes in production, yet it is the nature of production that will mostly determine the conditions of life within a society and hence its culture.

The bourgeois conception limits culture to the spiritual and ethical values of man. It was this conception of culture which prevailed at the Congress of Negro Writers and Artists in 1959. Speeches were delivered on semantics, vernacular literature, philosophy and religion, but none on economics or social structures.

A society based on private property is a society of classes.

In a society where one class dominates and exploits another, there are really two cultures; the culture of the dominant class, and the culture of the exploited class. Therefore, in a capitalist society there is the culture of the bourgeoisie, and that of the workers. The bourgeoisie limits the conception of culture so that it becomes the creation, and therefore the possession, of only a few, namely the intellectuals, who thus form a section of the bourgeoisie. In this way the creative work and activities of the masses are excluded.

Fanon said that culture was first and foremost the expression of a nation. While his central point, that the highest form of cultural manifestation of an oppressed people is through the liberation struggle, this does not flow from his definition of culture. In fact, the contested culture he talks about in a colonial situation is but a struggle between the oppressed and exploited classes and the colonizers who are the bourgeoisie. Here both the antagonistic classes make for the evolué. The oppressed and exploited need the intellectual not only because he is a part of them, but because they need his knowledge, skill and science in order to fight the oppressor.

Fanon defined culture in the course of his speech, but it is clear that he did not give much thought to it. While no objection could be raised in the fifties, as it did not affect his main point, it cannot be allowed to stand in the seventies. Fanon declared that culture is first and foremost the expression of a nation. But the nation grew up only at a certain stage in the development of man, and as a result of certain contradictions in society. Man existed in society, whether in a family or tribe long before the advent of the nation state. These pre-nation societies had cultures of their own. In fact, the merit that these cultures had over later cultures is that they were such as to embrace the entire people. The nation comes into history with the rise of a political institution, the state, so that it is frequently spoken of as the 'nation state'. But the rise of the nation state already implies two cultures, the culture of the ruling class and the culture of the exploited people. The nation state is the reflection of the fact that in society there are irreconcilable conflicts between the property-owning class and the dispossessed class.

At a certain stage of historical development, an epoch which we have already entered, class conflict will disappear with the elimination of the bourgeoisie. The nation state as we know it will disappear, but culture will not only continue, it will flower as never before. It will be the culture of an entire people, and on a higher level.

This faulty formulation of Fanon due to his lack of understanding of the history of mankind puts him alongside the evolués of the bourgeoisie, who regard the beginnings of cultural history as merely the spiritual culture of a nation. That is why he called black men the great 'absentees' of history. His formulation makes man the producer, an absentee of history although his culture ranges over thousands of years. It is thus not only the black man, but the pre-nation man, whom he shuts off from the universal cultural stream which is the proud and inspiring heritage of modern man.

Fanon obviously accepted the concept of the bourgeoisie, that culture is just the spiritual product which emanates from the intellectual. How else can we explain the astonishing statement that Africans have been the great 'absentees' of universal history? If culture is to be regarded as also embracing the activities of the producers as well, in the process of production, then it is the labour of the African people which laid the foundation for the culture of the modern bourgeoisie. In the mercantile capitalist period, it was unpaid slave labour in the sugar and rubber plantations which made capital accumulation possible. It is this immense reservoir of cheap, sweated labour that made it possible for the surplus to be extracted to build an industrial economy. It is this that gave impetus to bourgeois culture. But just as the bourgeoisie deny the oppressed and exploited workers and peasants the fruits of their labour, appropriating the surplus themselves, so their ideologists deny to the slaves and the exploited masses their contributions in the field of culture.

Fanon further idealized the nation and the state when

he said that in a colonial situation, culture, deprived of its two-fold support of the nation and the state, perishes and becomes moribund. The questions that Fanon should have posed are, which class controls the state, and whose ideas are dominant in the nation state? Within fifteen years of the Second Congress, over forty states in Africa gained independence, and in each a nation state has arisen. Thus, according to him, there should be a cultural renaissance in Africa. Yet nothing of the kind has happened, except in a few countries like Guinea and Tanzania. The reason for the absence of a blossoming of culture is that the class which controls the newly-independent countries is the bourgeoisie. It does so on behalf of the world dominant class, the international bourgeoisie. The rabid 'negrophiles' of Fanon's period have shown themselves to be enthusiastic Francophones. The international bourgeoisie controls the commanding heights of the economy and all the cultural institutions to disseminate its own ideas. It controls the press, the radio, the universities and the churches. By controlling the economy it is able to control most of the agencies of cultural life like the schools, colleges, research centres, and so on. All the people are left with are their traditional ceremonies, their paintings and their sculptures.

The condition for cultural independence then is economic independence. It is the conquest for the material basis of culture that will prepare the ground for spiritual independence in the fields of philosophy, science, politics and art. The national bourgeoisie has not been able to perform this task. This will fall on the shoulders of the working class. The real cultural revolution is therefore tied in with the socialist revolution.

Fanon declared that national culture under conditions of colonialism is a contested culture which the bourgeoisie tries systematically to destroy. But what was the content of this culture? Was it a culture, slave or feudal in content, riddled with class divisions, or was it tribal culture? If the former, then one falsifies history if one says that colonial domination arrested that culture. History shows that in general, feudal culture had become fossilized and static.

Marx graphically showed the former nature of it in writing about India : 'We must not forget that these idyllic village communities, inoffensive though they might appear, had always been the foundation of oriental despotism, that they restrained the human mind within the smallest possible compass, making it the unresisting tool of superstition, enslaving it under traditional rulers, depriving it of all grandeur and historical energies. . . we must not forget that this undignified, stagnatory, vegetative life, rendered murder into a religious rite in Hindustan . . . we must not forget that these village communities were contaminated by distinctions of caste and slavery that subjugated man to external circumstances instead of elevating man to become the sovereign of circumstances . . . formed a self developing social organism into a never changing natural destiny, thus bringing about a brutalizing worship of nature, exhibiting its degradation in the fact that man the sovereign of nature, fell down on his knees in adoration of Hanuman the monkey, and Sabbala the cow.'[4] Similarly, pre-colonial African societies, because the productive forces were poorly developed, were also subject to myths and superstitions.

In the period of colonial conquest, the western powers pillaged and plundered. Resistance by the people led to mass and savage slaughter. But the bourgeoisie during its rule has created more massive productive forces than have all the preceding generations together. In other words, colonial conquest had two sides, of which Fanon was only able to grasp one. That was the conquest which was accompanied by pillage, plunder and exploitation, and the attempted destruction of the cultures of the conquered peoples. But there was the other side, where capitalism attacked and threw into the dustbins of history the fossilized and the stagnant, which had dominated for centuries. Willy nilly, these societies drawn into the capitalist orbit would now be in a position to utilize the colossal productive forces unlocked by capitalism once they had dealt with capitalist exploitation and oppression. When that was achieved the societies would also be free from the tyranny of the once all-powerful nature, which had only grudgingly yielded its secrets to man over the centuries. In the liberation struggle against colonialism and neocolonialism it is imperative that the people learn to make use of scientific discoveries exploited by capitalism, and use them as instruments for liberation.

The form of a nation state may remain constant for centuries, but its content continues to change. The Russian state changed its content three times within a period of less than fifty years. Thus from feudalism, Russia passed through capitalism and into socialism within a short period. The socialist culture that is arising in the Soviet Union was only possible after the October Revolution of 1917, when the culture became proletarian, because the working class became the dominant class after the October 1917 revolution.

Verse, song and drama is not limited to singing about the beauties of nature, for the struggle for liberation has its own beauty and grandeur which have inspired some of the best poetry. Man in Vietnam is not only a producer, but also a soldier. Ho Chi Minh said that nothing was more precious than freedom and independence. The soldier becomes also a poet. This aspect of Vietnamese culture combines both the love for freedom, with love for production as well as love for the beautiful in nature. The poets of Vietnam have blossomed during the revolution. Here are two examples of their verses. The full and all rounded man not only thinks and feels, but also acts.

Hammocks hung high in heaven ...
The fairies of yore slept in silken hammocks,
Nowadays I hang mine as high as heaven,
Out of boredom the flies tossed about,
Soundly I sleep in the lap of hills and trees,
The fairies drifted with the clouds,
I dream of a ruse to envelop and wipe out the foe.

Cong Ham

Marching Troops ....
Nicest is the glow of youth,

Merriest is the send off for front bound lads,
Most boisterous is the rush of a post,
Through a dense net of fire cracking everywhere.

Most exciting is a combined attack,
Most precious is our peoples' love,
Flowers blooming goodbye when we start on a route,
Flowers smiling welcome when we return with glory.
Hong Thao

The Tet is celebrated in Vietnam with verse, song and dance not only because plants bud anew, but also because it is associated with glorious struggles of the Vietnamese against aggression and invasion. But the most glorious chapter of Vietnamese history may well be the Tet of 1968. This broke the spine of American imperialism. It was a fight which was part of a larger struggle between capitalism and socialism. What was involved was whether the man produced by a party committed to scientific socialism could withstand the merciless pounding of one of the most murderous machines of death and destruction yet evolved by man. Victory for the Vietnamese represents the triumph of socialist man over the forces of capitalism.

One feature of the struggle in independent African states in the field of ideas is whether science should triumph over superstitions and myths. The producers need the application of science not only in the fields of agriculture and industry, but also in the fields of sociology, history and politics. The people need science in order to liberate themselves. But only a socialist view of culture will be able to make them see the problems in their entirety and also serve as a guide to correct action.

Fanon's failure to look at culture as part of man's activities which are constantly in a process of change, and his inability to recognize that in a class society within a nation there are two cultures, flowed from his attachment to another fashionable philosophy, namely existentialism. The chief spokesman of modern existentialism at that time was Jean-Paul Sartre. If there was one living person to whom Fanon looked up to for inspiration as well as guidance it was to Sartre, who was then regarded as perhaps the leading thinker and novelist not only in France, but in the entire western world. The philosophy of existentialism was a challenge to the Marxist philosophy of dialectical materialism.

The merit of Marxism – Leninism is that its socialism is scientific. There were socialists and communists before Marx. More's Utopia visualized an ideal society where there would be complete equality and no oppression. But this socialism like that of Owen and Fourier was utopian because it was not based on understanding of the historical laws operating in society, which made socialism not only something desirable, but also inevitable.

In the twentieth century Marxism – Leninism has become the dominant trend of revolutionary workers and peasants because only political organizations basing themselves on its ideology have been able to conquer power from the bourgeoisie and at the same time been able to retain it. Besides, the Soviet Union, China, North Vietnam, North Korea, Albania and East European countries have showed the correctness of this theory for their revolutions were led by parties basing themselves on Marxism – Leninism. But just as in nature one has freaks which are exceptions, so too in society. Cuba proved an exception. But now it confirms the rule that only a party based on Marxism – Leninism is in a position to retain power once it has been seized from the bourgeoisie. There have been no military coups in truly socialist countries.

Sartre began his attack on dialectical materialism in earnest in 1946, with his essay on *Materialism and Revolution*. But some sixteen years later, he turned, and instead of repudiating it, said that existentialism was also aimed at supplementing and developing Marxism. This later position also contained logical problems.

Even if the existentialists were never able to comprehend Marxism fully, Marxists on the other hand, understanding the class from which this attack came, understood the existentialists. While modern existentialism retains its religious wing in Jasper and Marcel, its other branch is atheistic in orientation and this was represented by Sartre and Camus.

The intellectuals coming from the Second World War, where the old values had collapsed needed answers to burning questions about what went wrong. Marxism had the answers, and in fact the latest crises in capitalism had just confirmed their thesis that the bourgeoisie was mismanaging society. The chronic instability leading to wars was in fact inherent in the system, and capitalism could be overthrown by social action. Existentialism instead of turning the searchlight on capitalist society focused attention on the plight and problem of the individual. Sartre and his group attacked Marxism for dividing the world into the objective and subjective, and giving primary place to the objective. Marxism says that the subject becomes aware, that is, he gains knowledge as he conquers the object, the world around him. But the existentialists in the words of Sartre say, 'Man rises up in the world and defines himself afterwards'.[5]

But man is not the kind of animal Sartre would have us believe, but the social product of years of evolution. In these thousands of years he has acquired a vast body of knowledge, and experience. He has evolved social and political organizations, and brought into being new modes of production. To understand man today, it is necessary to understand his past. And it is only in understanding the process of his development that one can then begin to understand the processes which change man and society as a whole.

The existentialists pay a great deal of attention to the freedom of the individual and Sartre described freedom as a basic fact of man's existence. 'We represent,' says Sartre, 'freedom which chooses, but we could not choose to be free. We are doomed to freedom'.[6] In other words, actions and omissions are facets of this definition of freedom. Avoiding action, and refusing to act, according to him, is also action. Refusing to choose is as much a choice as choosing is.

Marx on the contrary, gave man a more creative role in his philosophy: 'Men make their own history, but they do not make it just as they please; they do not make it under circumstances chosen by themselves, but under circumstances directly found, given and transmitted from the past.'[7] Man's freedom thus consists in understanding what is before him in relation to what he is capable of. Man, for instance, longed for the freedom to go to the moon, but it remained merely a wish for centuries. It was only when he reached a certain stage of technological and scientific development and solved a number of problems with rockets in space that it was possible to realize this freedom.

The same could be said of a people under colonialism. They wish to rid themselves of oppression and to win their freedom. Marxists see that the national liberation movement was set in motion as a result of implanting the capitalist mode of production in the colonies. Once this happened, the structure of tribal and feudal economies inevitably collided with this new mode of production. This made the rise of the national movement and its conflict with imperialism inevitable. However, even when the objective factors and the contradictions are present it takes time before people realize this. In the process of understanding they use other means like inter-tribal unity, religious associations or just spontaneous uprisings to achieve their ends. Only through bitter experience can they finally embark on the right path.

The position of the existentialist was such that he valued his individual freedom more than anything else. He did not link up his freedom with freedom for the rest of society. Nor did he see that he could not really be free if the rest of society was in chains. Thus Simone de Beauvoir, Sartre's lifelong companion says: 'In our youth we felt close to the Communist party to the extent that its negativism harmonized with our anarchism. We looked forward to the defeat of capitalism, but not to the coming of socialist society which, we thought, would deprive us of our liberty.'[8] Evidently, she preferred individual liberty under capitalism, to freedom for the oppressed and exploited under socialism. And Sartre wrote in his notebook in 1939, when Stalin concluded a temporary pact with Hitler : 'Here I am cured of socialism, if I ever needed to be cured of it.'[9] However, Sartre's hatred of capitalism was deep. In one article he said : 'In the name of principles which it had inculcated in me, in the name of its humanism, and its humanities, in the name of liberty, equality and fraternity, I vowed a hatred for the bourgeoisie that would last to the end of my days.'[10]

Marx noted in the Communist manifesto, that the inexorable workings of the laws of capitalism with its anarchic competition rendered bankrupt certain layers of the bourgeoisie who then were thrown into the ranks of the working class. Likewise, some intellectuals revolt to join the parties of the working class. Sartre throws bricks at the capitalist system. But it is an individual act. He does not join the working-class movements aiming at the overthrow of the capitalist system. As a detached intellectual he sympathized with the working class and the oppressed colonial people. On a number of issues he lent his weight and authority to their cause. But he never identified himself completely. For his existentialist philsophy made him determined at all costs to retain his personal liberty.

But with Fanon, there could be no midway position. He was black, and therefore part of the seething mass of the oppressed colonial people who were demanding their freedom. Sartre could retire into his ivory tower and continue writing learned books on philosophy, but not Fanon. Every time a Vietnamese was shot, or an Algerian was tortured, he felt the pain through his own body. For Fanon there could be no escape.

Existentialism made its appearance when capitalism was becoming senile and decadent, and when it was being rocked by a series of crises. Existentialism reflected this, and its philosophy of the despair, fear, hopelessness and the purposelessness of life, found support from the bewildered intellectuals of post-war Europe. Death was one of the subjects discussed often by existentialists. Yet only a century earler the ideologists of capitalism were full of optimism. Said the philosopher Spinoza : 'The free man thinks of everything but his death; his wisdom is not death, but pondering on life'.

Fanon on the other hand, was linked with a world-wide movement, embracing three awakening continents. The sun for them was rising, and not declining. Before his very eyes, he could see the epoch of colonial uprisings beginning to enter a decisive phase. The millions of the oppressed and exploited who seemingly had been dormant for centuries had awakened and had begun to settle accounts with imperialism and capitalism in its super-monopoly stage. The oppressed millions then were full of optimism and hope for the future, for the middle of the twentieth century was in fact becoming the era of the 'common man'.

Fanon joined this mainstream of teeming humanity on the march by his identification and participation in the Algerian Revolution. But he did so without repudiating the philosophy of existentialism which was completely alien to the Revolution. But then, this was Fanon's own contradiction, and even before he could work out a philosophic position which would correspond with his political activities in the Algerian revolution, he died. His personal contradiction was never resolved. It is perhaps the final irony that the Preface to Fanon's best known book, *The Wretched of the Earth,* is written by Sartre, thereby linking his name with existentialism, a concept in ultimate contradiction with Fanon's part in the Algerian revolution and the image projected of him by those who claim to be his followers.

4
PSYCHIATRY AND POLITICS

The function of a social structure is to set up institutions to serve man's needs. A society that drives its members to desperate solutions is a nonviable society, a society to be replaced.[1]

FANON graduated as a doctor in 1951. At that time he cherished the illusion that he could best serve the people by practising medicine, healing and ministering to the sick, and that it was simply a question of where he could make the greatest contribution. He practised psychotherapy first in the hospital at Saint Ylie, just outside Lyon. But in 1952 moved to the hospital at Saint Alban where he worked under the direction of Professor Tosquelles. The latter had become famous for the introduction of many new theories and techniques in the diagnosis and treatment of the mentally sick. Tosquelles emphasized the need for the psychiatrist to study the total behaviour of each patient in the context of his home and social environment. The whole atmosphere at Saint Alban was relaxed and informal. Patients were encouraged to engage in craft work, painting, gardening and many other group activities designed to make them feel part of a community, to teach them skills, and to give them outlets for constructive and positive work.

Fanon as a young and newly qualified practitioner was greatly influenced by Tosquelles and fully agreed with the importance attached to examining the social and political background of each patient. He had already come to know Algerian patients in France and was intensely interested in the physical and psychological effects of their double oppression as victims of colonialism and racism.

In what he calls the 'North African Syndrome', he has described the kind of situation which arose when a North African sought medical attention in France: 'Except in urgent cases – an intestinal occlusion, wounds, accidents – the North African arrives enveloped in vagueness. He has an ache in his belly, in his back, he has an ache everywhere. He suffers miserably, his face is eloquent, he is obviously suffering.

' "What's wrong, my friend?"

"I'm dying, *monsieur le docteur*." His voice breaks imperceptibly.
"Where do you have pain?"
"Everywhere, *monsieur le docteur*".'²

The French doctor, more often than not, would conclude that the North African was a malingerer. In reaching this conclusion the doctor was, even if subconsciously, influenced by the fact that he was a member of a 'master race', and the patient was a member of a 'subject race'. The doctor was white, the patient black. Having accepted the dominant ideas of the ruling class, the doctor looked at the Algerian as he did the colons, French settlers in Algeria – with contempt. Racialism had raised its ugly head and had barred that delicate and vital human relationship between doctor and patient. The dominant ideas of the ruling class in capitalist society are such that those who produce its wealth are frequently regarded as lazy, good-for-nothing loafers. Thus the French doctors believed the Algerians complained of imaginary ailments in order to get off work, or to enjoy the comfort of a spell in hospital, and often failed to diagnose the root cause of the perfectly genuine suffering of their patients.

Fanon and Tosquelles belonged to the new school of medicine that went beyond the once accepted norm that where there are symptoms one must look for lesions; and if there is no specific lesion, no specific wound or pain, then there is no sickness. The modern school to which Fanon belonged, believed that there must be an all round examination of the patient. His case history must also include his life history, and his occupation as well as his environment should also be taken into account. Last but not least, the patient's sense of security or sense of insecurity should be noted. Apart from the obvious sympathy he had with the patient, his broader examination of the patient's problem led him to the conclusion that the root of his sickness lay in the oppressive society in which he lived. More often than not, it was his lack of shelter and clothes that drove him to hospital and created a mental breakdown. He noted that in winter months, when there was severe cold, the hospitals in France were unusually crowded. He understood that behind the patient's feeling of sickness all over the body lay the patient's feeling of insecurity. That was why the patient did not want to leave hospital and face what he regarded as the hell outside. The Algerians in France died a daily death. They had become neurotic and were in need of psychiatric treatment. This was how he explained the apparant paradox of a man 'with robust muscles who tells us in his truly broken voice, "Doctor I'm going to die".'[3]

These observations were made by Fanon in a penetrating article published in *L'Esprit* in February 1952. At that stage he believed that this section of oppressed humanity, driven to neurosis, could be saved from its sickness within the framework of the French colonial system: 'there is work to be done over there, human work, that is, work which is the meaning of a home. Not that of a room or a barrack building. It means that over the whole territory of the French nation (the metropolis and the French Union), there are tears to be wiped away, inhuman attitudes to be fought, condescending ways of speech to be ruled out, men to be humanized'.[4]

These were the conclusions of a young, newly-qualified doctor attending to his first patients. Fanon was full of enthusiasm and thought he had the problem solved. It was this idealism which made him apply in 1953 for the post of chef de service of the largest psychiatric hospital in Algeria at Blida-Joinville. He believed that it was possible to alleviate the sufferings of the Algerians by medical means and he intended to introduce the methods of treatment used at Saint Alban. The post was offered to him, and in November 1953 he and his wife Josie, left France for Algeria. Fanon had married Josie Dublé, a white woman, in 1952. A progressive thinker and a political activist, Josie had considerable intellectual influence on her husband. She was to become just as committed to the struggle of the Algerian people as Fanon himself. After his death she renounced her French citizenship, choosing to live with her two sons permanently in Algeria where she continues her political work.

Information is scanty about Fanon's day to day work at the Blida-Joinville Hospital. But it is possible to deduce the frustrations and disappointments he must have experienced, dealing with the mentally sick in the conditions of Algeria at that time. Before he left France he had already diagnosed the malady of many of the Algerian patients with whom he had come into contact as closely related to their political, social and economic environment, stemming from their condition as a 'subject race'. In Algeria itself, face to face with the realities of colonialism, his diagnosis was confirmed, and he came to the conclusion that the people's condition could not be cured by medical treatment alone. Revolutionary change to end colonial rule and to make possible a radical change in society would provide the only meaningful solution. He had found in Algeria a 'systematized dehumanization'.[5]

Conditions at Blida-Joinville when Fanon arrived in November 1953 to take up his appointment were far from good. Methods were old-fashioned, there was over-crowding and an acute shortage of doctors and nurses. The hospital which had been built to accommodate 970 patients housed more than 2,000, and in September 1954 there was a waiting list of a further 850. Coping as best they could were some five or six doctors who were grossly over-worked.

Fanon at once set to work to transform the life of the hospital, introducing the socio-therapeutic methods of hospitals in France. Within a week of his arrival fundamental changes had been made. Fanon had found difficult patients tied to their beds. He ordered their immediate release. No patient was to be subjected to de-humanizing and de-personalizing treatment. They were grouped as at Saint Alban in small units consisting of some ten to twelve patients, and were provided with opportunities to engage in all kinds of work therapy. The object was to end the patient's sense of isolation and alienation and to make each one feel part of a community with a constructive role to play in it. More nurses were recruited, particularly male nurses and they were given increased responsibility. For Fanon considered the nurses a vital link between doctor and patient.

To disseminate information about the new methods of treatment, the reorganization of the life of the hospital, and also to provide work for the patients, Fanon arranged for the publication of a hospital newspaper, *Notre Journal*. There was a special section in the newspaper for each ward, and every week Fanon wrote the Editorial. Doctors and nurses contributed, and occasionally a patient. Fanon hoped that the newspaper would be a vehicle through which staff and patients would express their opinions and ideas on how to improve the life of the hospital. But results were disappointing not only as regards *Notre Journal*, but concerning other activities and new methods of therapy introduced by Fanon and the small group of doctors who worked with him. There was particular difficulty in getting male patients to respond, and this led Fanon and his colleagues to re-examine the whole basis of their methods to discover why it was that techniques which had proved to be very successful in France failed in Algeria. For this it was necessary to study the historical, cultural and social background of the patients.

In 1954, after working for a year at Blida-Joinville, Fanon and a colleague published 'La Socialthérapie dans un service d'hommes musulmans' (sociotherapy in a ward of Muslim males). In this article they described the difficulties encountered in trying to apply techniques and theories derived from one culture to another. Fanon was rapidly coming to the conclusion that there was a direct relationship between colonialism and the psychological condition of colonizers and the colonized. As a psychiatrist dealing with the mentally sick within a colonial society he was being called upon to help men and women adjust to that environment. But this was something which he was not prepared to try to do. The cure for the ills of colonialism was to end colonialism. In other words, the cure lay in finding a political and not a medical solution. Having diagnosed colonialism as the basic cause of the mental sickness of

Algerians, Fanon was but a short step away from active commitment to the Algerian national liberation movement.

It was not only the colonized, but the colonizer who suffered mental illness. Fanon saw many cases of mental breakdown among police agents which could be directly attributed to the brutalizing effects of colonialism.

'They hit their children hard, for they think they are still with Algerians.

They threaten their wives, for "I threaten and execute all day long".

They do not sleep, because they hear the cries and the moans of their victims.'[6]

Are such men, Fanon asks, suffering from a revolt of moral conscience? After armed struggle broke out in Algeria, police methods became more and more ruthless. There was a big rise in the number of cases of insanity among police agents during the first quarter of 1956. The symptoms were insomnia, nightmares, threats of suicide, and in some cases the inflicting of severe injury on their wives and children.

In 1956, Fanon decided to resign from Blida Hospital. In his letter of resignation sent to the Resident Minister in 1956, he made it clear that the grim realities of colonial life had shattered all his illusions that it was possible to bring sanity and mental health to an entire oppressed people without political independence. He had for nearly three years placed himself wholly at the service of the country and of the men who inhabited it. 'There is not a parcel of my activity that has not had as its objective the unanimously hoped-for emergence of a better world.'[7] In actual practice he found brutality, harshness and repression. 'The degree of alienation of the inhabitants of this country appears to me frightening.'[8] He added : 'I owe it to myself to affirm that the Arab, permanently an alien in his own country, lives in a state of absolute depersonalization'.[9] He was shocked at the severe measures taken against striking workers, for 'to punish the workers who went out on strike on 5 July 1956, is a measure which, literally, strikes me as irrational'.[10] He reminded the Resident Minister that 'fear has not struck me as being the dominant mood of the strikers. Rather there was the inevitable determination to bring about, in calm and silence, a new era of peace and dignity'.[11] Fanon was in fact acknowledging that he was wasting his time at the Blida-Joinville Hospital, for his hard and painstaking work would never yield positive results as 'the social structure existing in Algeria was hostile to any attempt to put the individual back where he belonged'.[12]

Fanon's resignation from government service and his expulsion from Algeria in January 1957 meant the loss of a potential liberal. The function of western liberalism is to oil the capitalist machinery of exploitation, to loosen a tight screw here or there, or to remove a tight lid to prevent an explosion. The liberal achieves a few reforms so that the machine is given a longer lease of life and rebels do not become revolutionaries. But Fanon, instead of mellowing with big responsibility as head of a department, had joined the Algerian national liberation movement.

There was more to Fanon's resignation than the reasons given in his letter of resignation to the Resident Minister. It was more than a question of breaking with French colonialism and of refusing to be a collaborator with it. He was already identifying himself with forces aimed at overthrowing French colonialism. Before he took the post he was able to detect the rumblings of revolution. The Algerian nationalist movement, after years of reformist and legal activity, was entering a new phase. The first shots had been fired when Fanon was already in Algeria, and this beginning of the armed phase of the revolution immediately brought about a separation of forces. There could be no more sitting on the fence. Either one was with the Algerian people against French colonialism, or with French colonialism and against the Algerian people.

Fanon had no trouble with his conscience, or about where he belonged and which side he should support. He was drawn into the struggle, for the people of Algeria were doing what he himself had advocated in his first book, *Black Skin, White Masks*. His hospital ward soon became a haven for militants of the F L N (National Liberation Front), who wanted temporary shelter. All they had to do was to feign insanity, and then get the respite and protection they needed. In this sense, Blida Hospital became a base area in enemy-held territory. But this situation could not last for ever. Fanon had already attracted the attention of the authorities who had become suspicious of his activities. He resigned before matters came to a head. The Resident Minister too was not sorry to lose Fanon. His political leanings had become an embarrassment.

Fanon was not a man for half measures. He would throw himself wholeheartedly into a cause which he believed to be right. In Blida Hospital he had worked tirelessly. He had given all he had because he believed that this was the noblest and most humanitarian work open to him. Three years later, he realized that this was a mistake for he was serving to revive a rotten and decadent system. After November 1956, he turned to the Algerian national movement which had already entered its armed phase. It was his belief that the new order that he longed for would emerge from the outcome of this struggle. He plunged into it with the same zeal and dedication that had characterized his work at Blida Hospital.

5
FANON AND THE FLN

During the colonial period the people are called upon to fight against oppression; after national liberation, they are called upon to fight against poverty, illiteracy and underdevelopment. The struggle, they say, goes on. The people realize that life is an unending contest.[1]

AFTER resigning from the Psychiatric Department of the Blida Hospital, Fanon went first to France and then in 1957 to Tunis. In Tunis he taught in the University and ran courses for the general public on various aspects of psychiatry and politics. In 1959, for example, he lectured on 'The social psychology of the black world'. But eventually, the Tunisian government stopped the courses. Fanon thought this was owing to pressure from the French government.

During this time, Fanon became a militant member of the F L N. But he had not abandoned his medical work. He practised psychiatry under the assumed name of 'Dr Fares' at the Manouba clinic and the Centre Neuropsychiatrique de Jour de Tunis. In addition, he worked in F L N medical centres and clinics along the Moroccan and Tunisian frontiers. There he saw at first hand the human consequences of the Algerian war of liberation. There were patriots who had been beaten up and tortured by the colonial police, and as a result some of them had become physical and mental wrecks. In his book *The Wretched of the Earth*, Fanon has described the case histories of these patients and the various types of torture which many of them endured. A particularly atrocious torture was the injection of water into the prisoner's mouth accompanied by an enema of soapy water inserted at high pressure. This torture was the cause of a large number of deaths resulting from perforations of the intestine, gaseous embolisms and peritonitis. There were wounded soldiers, refugee women and children, and many patients who suffered from various states of depression and anxiety. Fanon wrote about them under the title 'Colonial war and mental disorders'. He concluded that Africans must not try to imitate Europeans or aspire to catch up with Europe: 'Comrades, we must turn over a new leaf, we must work out new concepts, and try to set afoot a new man'.[2]

Fanon worked harder in Tunisia than in any previous period of his life. The psychiatric work which had led him to active participation in the Algerian national liberation struggle had also resulted in a renewed interest in writing. For Fanon found that his skills both as a doctor and as a writer were urgently needed by the F L N. While in Tunis between September 1957 and January 1960, he wrote for *El Moudjahid*, the newspaper of the F L N, and for *Résistance Algérienne*, the organ of the A L N (Algerian liberation army). Articles in *El Moudjahid* were published anonymously, but Fanon's widow, Josie, has identified many of those written by her husband. They show clearly the growing maturity of Fanon's thought, and his awareness that the Algerian struggle formed part of the world-wide struggle of the colonized. This was inseparable from the fight to achieve the total liberation and unification of the entire African continent.

When Fanon arrived in Tunis, the Algerian Revolution had entered the armed phase after years of legal and constitutional struggle against French colonialism, which had led the people into a political cul-de-sac. It was at that time drawing increasing external support from radical intellectuals of the west, as well as from Arab countries. It registered an important diplomatic victory when it was invited to send a delegation to the historic Bandung Conference of 1955 where African and Asian countries met together for the first time, and where the basis was laid for the non-aligned movement. It was there that a broad strategy was formulated to eliminate imperialism.

It was possible for Fanon to identify himself with the F L N for it was a mass movement. Article Five of its Statute said that every Algerian man or woman who was fighting for the objectives of the organization, in accordance with the rules currently in force, and who fulfilled all his obligations to the organization, was qualified to be a member of the F L N. While practising as a doctor at the Blida Hospital, Fanon had shown by his actions that he was more than a mere sympathizer with the Algerian revolutionary cause. He had taken risks like any other member of the F L N in giving sanctuary to F L N members. His inclusion in the F L N meant that the organization was admitting 'revolutionary outsiders' who had identified themselves with the cause.

The F L N declaration of 1 November 1954 calling for the recognition of Algeria's independence was the culmination of considerable nationalist activity going back to 1925 when Messali Hadj founded in Paris the Etoile Nord Africaine. In 1931, the association of *ulema* was formed by Sheikh Ben Badis. This was a cultural organization designed to spread the Arabic language and culture throughout Algeria. Under French colonial rule, Arabic was taught only as a second language in the schools, French being the official language of Algeria. This was the cause of much resentment since it was felt that the Algerian personality was being submerged, and Algerians were being lured into the expectation of becoming assimilated Europeans. Ben Badis sought to prevent this alienation of Algerians from their cultural heritage.

During the mid-1930s, Ferhat Abbas emerged as a nationalist leader. The parties he formed in 1938, 1944 and 1946 made increasingly nationalist demands, but called for reforms rather than for immediate independence. In 1943 in his Manifesto of the Algerian People, Ferhat Abbas demanded self-determination and the recognition of Arabic as the national language of Algeria. The following year he formed the A M L, the Amis du Manifeste de la Liberté.

Meantime, the Parti du Peuple Algérien (P P A) had been founded in 1937. Ten years later, the Mouvement pour le Triomphe des Libertés Démocratiques (M T L D) was founded by Messali Hadj. There developed from this a revolutionary wing which began to function as an underground organization. This wing established a secret section called the Organization Secréte (O S). Among its leading members were Ben Bella, Mohammed Khider and Ait Mohammed. This was to be the first stage in the formation of the Comité Révolutionnaire pour l'Unité et l'Action (C R U A) formed in 1954. The C R U A was the direct predecessor of the F L N. A month before the first shots were fired in the Algerian liberation war C R U A dissolved itself to launch the F L N.

Members of the O S believed that armed struggle was necessary if the national liberation struggle was to succeed. They saw that non-violent methods had achieved virtually nothing. French promises of reform and assimilation had proved false. There was increasing unemployment, continuing European domination of the economic life of the country, and very little educational opportunity for the majority of the Algerian people. Furthermore, to proceed via the ballot box had been shown to be a hopeless exercise. It was generally agreed that the elections of 1948 were fraudulent.

The O S was at first urban-based but it soon spread to the countryside. Although the O S extended its network throughout Algeria, it was particularly strong in the Aures and Kabyle regions. Ben Bella distinguished himself as a leader of the O S when he led a daring raid on the Oran Post Office. He was caught and imprisoned in 1950 but escaped from Blida prison and went to Cairo.

Time was on the side of the O S. A marked change had taken place in the attitude of the Algerian people towards the national liberation struggle. Those who had considered the way forward lay through the ballot box had been disillusioned by the rigging of elections and no longer thought it would be possible to achieve political independence employing only constitutional methods.

The Second World War had destroyed the myth of the invincibility of the French army. Algerians who had fought side by side with French soldiers found that after the war they were no longer treated on terms of equality. In May 1945 there had been demonstrations in Setif, and at one stage the flag of Algeria had been raised. There were clashes between Algerians and colons. To teach the Algerians a lesson, the French brought in troops and Algerians estimate that some 45,000 Algerians were killed. It was one of the most barbarous massacres of a colonized people. But it sowed the seeds of the future armed struggle. From that moment, the Algerians became convinced that the only language the French understood was the language of force.

When armed struggle was launched in Algeria in 1954, the F L N defined its goals as: 'National independence in a north African framework, restoration of an Algerian state, sovereign, democratic and social within the framework of Islamic principles'. Fundamental liberties would be respected without distinction of race and colour. Later statutes of the F L N clarified this and stated that the fundamental objective was the restoration of the sovereign Algerian state and the building of a democratic republic. On the question of its future programme the F L N stated that it fought for the establishment in Algeria of 'a free society based on political and social democracy'. It fought to give the resources of Algeria, and their management, to the Algerian people.

Despite the temporary setback after the arrest of Ben Bella the O S was able to continue its activities. The French were never able to destroy its network particularly in the rural areas. By early 1954 not only did the leaders regroup themselves but they also extended their activities. It was at the beginning of 1954 that C R U A was formed. This organization consisted of 22 members and an executive of five. They were Ben M'Hidi, Mohammed Boudaif, Moustefa Ben Boulaid, Mourad Didouche, and Rabah Bitat. Four others who were not present were co-opted. These were Belkacem Krim, Hocine Ait Ahmed, Ben Bella and Mohammed Khider. These became the historic 'Nine'. C R U A fixed the date for the beginning of the armed struggle as well as the name of the new organization which would launch it. This was the Front de Libération Nationale (F L N).

The F L N was born on 1 November 1954 when simultaneous attacks were made on French installations and police headquarters. In Algiers a petrol depot belonging to an oil monopoly was blown up. These attacks fired the imagination of the people and almost overnight the F L N was seen to be a national movement. The French realized by the scale of the attacks and their synchronization that they were faced with not merely a rising of a handful of 'terrorists', but with a rebellion of the masses. Within a year the French army in Algeria was increased from 120,000 men to 400,000. In addition it had at its command some 200,000 puppet troops.

The F L N issued a stirring call to the Algerian people through its Manifesto which proclaimed its aims and objectives and the methods of struggle to be employed. It aimed to restore the sovereign democratic state of Algeria within the framework of the principles of Islam by respecting the basic rights of man without distinction of race or creed. It recognized that the struggle would be a long and arduous one but the outcome was certain. Regarding methods the words of the Manifesto were clear: 'According to our revolutionary principles and taking into account the external and internal situation, we shall continue to fight by every means until we realize our aims'. Significantly, the Manifesto made it clear that the struggle was for national liberation and was not against the French people but against French domination. The Manifesto declared that French interests, cultural and economic, which had been honestly acquired would be respected. All Frenchmen wishing to remain in Algeria were to be given the choice of retaining their French citizenship, in which case they would be treated as foreigners, or of becoming Algerian citizens. The F L N Manifesto went on to dissociate itself with any of the other organizations which had been formed in the past to conduct the liberation movement. The only enemy of the F L N was declared to be 'hostile and blind colonialism'. In rejecting the old political parties the F L N declared that the former leaders of the national movement had through their policies almost destroyed the movement: 'Our national movement weakened by years of routine and inactivity, badly directed and deprived of the indispensable support of public opinion and overtaken by events is gradually disintegrating'.

The programme was broad and national. It was capable of attracting all the oppressed layers of the Algerian population from feudal landowners and the rising bourgeoisie to workers and peasants. Compared with some of the slogans put out by the P P A it was moderate. For example, it did not demand 'land for the tiller'. But in 1954 the important point was to get the maximum unity and to establish as broad a front as possible. There was no mention in the Manifesto of the kind of society to be built in Algeria after the defeat of French colonialism. It was not that the Nine had no views on this. But they were convinced that the issue would resolve itself with the growth of the political consciousness of the people resulting from the armed struggle. The first priority was to emerge from the inertia and passivity of the reformist political arena and to adopt positive militant action.

The reformist leadership of the nationalist organizations committed to constitutional methods of struggle initially condemned the outbreak of armed struggle. Messali Hadj and Ferhat Abbas gave pledges to France and completely dissociated themselves with the F L N. The spineless Algerian Communist Party condemned the outbreak of fighting as 'adventurism'. But the ordinary people were delighted as they made the struggle their own. The Manifesto calling for independence as well as positive action towards the attainment of this aim caught their imagination. Here were people sacrificing their lives and careers for the noble cause of independence. How different from those who had used the support of the people to build up a career for themselves. Thanks to the support the F L N received further attacks were made. The colonial government arrested leading militants of the M T L D and within a month 1,200 were rounded up. When this did not bring the desired result they banned the organization and locked up the older reformist leaders.

The F L N had launched armed struggle using the military strategy of guerrilla warfare. While not neglecting the towns it focused its chief area of activity in the rural areas, the weakest link in the colonialist system. Two months after the beginning of the armed phase the F L N leadership reviewed the situation. On the debit side it recognized that the arrest of some of its militants had been a severe setback. It had also lost at least 42 members who had been killed in action. However, on the positive side it had scored two major victories. First, it had established the armed wing of the F L N. This was the A L N, the National Liberation Army. Secondly, the mass of the Algerian people knew that the F L N existed and that armed struggle on a national scale had broken out.

At the beginning of 1955 there was a sharp rise in the number of guerrilla attacks. Tactics of sabotage and ambush were used on a large scale. Prime targets were army convoys, military barracks, and communication systems. Isolated farms of the colons were also attacked. During this year the A L N was able to standardize its equipment and was even able to obtain anti-aircraft guns. On the political front, some of the well-known collaborators including Ferhat Abbas began to talk openly about a sovereign Algerian parliament. In December 1955, Ferhat and his followers resigned from the Assembly. By this time, Ferhat Abbas was already in touch with the F L N. His example was followed by other political leaders who had previously supported policies of collaboration with the French government.

The centre of the struggle shifted in 1955 to the north Constantine region where French colons owned large farms. French paratroopers had massacred hundreds of innocent civilians in this area as reprisal for A L N attacks. On 20 August 1955, the A L N launched a general offensive in north Constantine and within a short period they liberated twelve villages. Large numbers of colons panicked and abandoned their farms.

With the experience of Vietnam the French realized that they were dealing not with just a few groups of terrorists but with a national uprising. However, they had still to learn the lesson of Dien Bien Phu. Instead of negotiating with the F L N, the French doubled and then trebled the strength of their armed forces. By the end of 1955 the French army of about 50,000 men had swollen to some 190,000. Evidently the French government believed that the only way to suppress a national rebellion was to parade a massive show of force. Against the increasing guerrilla activities the French launched a series of massive counter-insurgency campaigns. These involved the use of thousands of troops supported by aircraft and even warships. These 'search and destroy' compaigns were aimed at wiping out guerrilla bases and at the same time razing to the ground those villages which supported the peasants. Outwardly, France gave the impression that the revolution had been contained. But it gave the game away by continually extending the state of emergency or the 'prohibited zones' to more parts of Algeria. In the middle of 1955 the colonial government extended the state of emergency to the regions of Constantine, Algiers and Oran. Twelve months later, the whole of Algeria came under martial law.

The French evolved barbarous methods to subdue a people determined to be free. One of the most notorious was the system of collective punishment. The A L N had dared to attack north Constantine. As punishment, French troops were sent to the region of Philippeville to inflict mass punishment. This was a combined operation of army, air force and navy. Innocent people were collected and herded into a stadium in the town of Philippeville and massacred in cold blood. But atrocities such as these had the effect of further uniting the Algerian people.

At about this time there began to appear the first signs of division among the French people. An anti-war mood began to show among the French youth. There were demonstrations by soldiers and young people in Rouen, Toulon and Valence. Many of the soldiers were veterans of the Vietnam war, and did not want to become involved in yet another unjust colonial war.

At the end of the first fourteen months of armed struggle the F L N had begun to move from the mountains to the plains. A major part of Constantine and the Aures region as well as an important zone in Oran had been liberated. In north Constantine the peasants were able to occupy the farms vacated by the colons. In these regions the F L N implemented agrarian reform through peasant committees which apportioned land to the peasants. In these and in other liberated areas it sought to improve the standard of living of the peasants by ensuring fair distribution of resources.

The F L N was a broad front which included people from all classes. It did not believe in a policy of uniting with existing organizations. It was different, however, in the case of the Union of Algerian Students (U G E M A). This organization was formed in 1955 and was a branch of the F L N. Its function was twofold. It had on the one hand to conduct a legal struggle, and at the same time to channel the most militant students to join the maquis in the forests and hills. From the time of its formation till its dissolution by the French in 1958, U G E M A played an important part in spreading the F L N Manifesto and making known the progress of the struggle to the Algerian people and to the workers and youth of metropolitan France. Members of U G E M A also collected funds for the F L N, and many gave up their studies and joined the A L N. Within a year of its formation U G E M A was able to call on students to go on strike. There was a very good response. The French took swift action and arrested the leaders. Many students fled either to the rural areas or went to Cairo, Tunis or Morocco. When the authorities finally banned the organization in 1958, U G E M A had already gone underground.

Another organization which fully supported the F L N was the General Union of Algerian Workers (U G T A), formed in 1956. This was set up in opposition to the feeble, reformist trade union organization which was linked with the French trade union movement. Members of U G T A mobilized urban workers in support of the F L N so that working-class areas of the towns became F L N strongholds and centres of urban guerrilla warfare. The activities alarmed the French for they well knew the power of an awakening working class. Through an agent provocateur the French arranged for a bomb to be exploded near to the headquarters of U G T A, and this gave the authorities an excuse to arrest some of the leaders. But far from frightening the workers, the organization called on them to strike in support of their leaders. On 1 November 1956, the FLN called for a general strike. Assisting the FLN and directly mobilizing the workers for this historic day were members of UGTA. Realizing the intimate connection between the FLN and UGTA, the French banned UGTA in 1958.

Such was the pressure exerted by the Algerian revolution that every section of the people and every organization was compelled sooner or later to make clear its position regarding the FLN. There could be no sitting on the fence. This made it difficult for France to find puppets. Open and die-hard collaborators became fewer, and some of them were executed by the fidayeen. Ferhat Abbas shrewdly decided that rather than try to fight the FLN it was better to join the bandwagon and to try to capture the organization from within.

The rapid growth of the FLN and ALN brought to the fore a number of important political and military organizational problems. For instance, where did the supreme political, administrative and military authority lie? Some of the FLN and ALN leaders had been killed, while others like Ben Bella and Ait Ahmed had been captured by the French. From a guerrilla force concerned mainly with sabotage and ambushes the ALN had developed into a regular army able to engage the colonial forces at battalion strength. Was independence to bring about fundamental change in the socio-economic structure of Algeria, or was it to be for the masses simply a question of changing masters? The direction in which the Algerian revolution proceeded would depend on which class led it. The failure of the Communist Party of Algeria to become part of the revolution weakened the proletarian base of the FLN, while the joining of the FLN by Ferhat Abbas and his friends strengthened its bourgeois content. The strength of the bourgeois section of the FLN lay in the external leadership. Being divorced from direct contact with workers and peasants, and with the guerrillas, it was possible for the right wing of the bourgeois section to corrupt certain leaders and to arrange for the assassination of others who could not be corrupted. The weakness of the bourgeoisie lay inside the country. Either they were not known by the large majority of the guerrillas, or they were distrusted by them.

The original F L N leadership was not elected. But by 1956 a stage in the struggle had been reached when it became necessary to devise machinery of power and authority, and to choose leaders which the people knew and trusted. For this purpose a conference was held in August 1956 in the Soumman Valley, a liberated area in the Aures. This settled the vital question of where supreme authority lay. The Conseil National de la Révolution (C N R A) was created. It was to consist of 17 full members and another 17 associate members. An executive committee was also formed known as the Co-ordinating and Executive Council (C C E). Members of these two organizations were elected and the choice of members showed that power was in the hands of nationalist revolutionaries who formed the O S and who had launched the revolution. Their hands were further strengthened by a resolution which stated that supreme authority lay in the internal sector and not the external. The supremacy of the internal wing over the external meant that the formulation of general strategy for the revolution as well as the political questions related to it would be in the hands of people who were directly involved in the fighting.

The Soumman Conference was the most representative conference that the Algerian national movement was to hold. Representatives of both the external and internal leadership were in attendance. The conference quickly got down to discussing the burning problems which had arisen as a result of the armed struggle. Members considered French imperialist strategy and the failure of existing political organizations such of the M T L D and the Communist Party of Algeria. The aims of the F L N were re-stated and a proper relationship was established between the political and the military, as well as between the external and the internal leadership. The military leadership was to be subordinate to the political. Not only was the existing strategy of the revolution analysed, but the future course in broad outline was also formulated. For in order to mobilize a strong periphery of supporters and sympathizers for the struggle, particular attention had to be paid to radicals like Sartre and the French liberal establishment. The Conference also considered the question of mobilizing the Jewish minority in Algeria for the struggle. Of particular significance was the analysis of forces which were the mainstays of the revolution. It noted that the massive participation of peasants and agricultural labourers had shown the popular character of Algerian resistance. This clearly indicates that there was a strong trend within the Algerian national movement which wanted to transform the national movement from one aiming solely at independence to one which aimed to change the social system by incorporating the demand of the peasants for land as an integral part of the programme. This would have turned the Algerian national movement from being not only against French imperialism but also against feudalism.

The democratic character of a national movement depends precisely on the cardinal question of whether it incorporates the demands of the peasantry for land. The Soumman Conference, however, did not incorporate the demand for land, and the ending of feudalism as one of its aims. However, the Conference noted the role of urban elements, students and workers, in raising the political consciousness of the masses. 'The presence of city elements with political maturity and experience under the leadership of the F L N have made it possible to politicize the backward regions. The contribution of female and male students have been highly useful in the political, administrative and medical fields.'

Within twenty months the French administration, despite the presence of almost one million French and puppet troops, had disintegrated in the countryside. It was not possible for the French to rule through its puppets or its institutions designed to suppress the people. From the ashes of colonial administration arose new organs of power 'People's Assemblies'. The Soumman Conference analysed this development and stated: 'The general Councils, municipal councils and the djemaas have disappeared ... due to the resignation of a great many officials, colonial assistants, and paid rural policemen. Due to the lack of applicants and people to replace them, the French administration has been disorganized and the skeleton administration ... finds no support among the people'. The meaning of this was clear: 'The slow but inexorable disintegration of French administration has made the birth and development of the system of dual power possible. A revolutionary administration with secret djemaas and organization is already in being, controlling supplies, the collection of taxes, the administration of justice, the recruiting of moudjahidenes (freedom fighters), security services and intelligence'. The revolution was already creating a state within a state.

As might be expected, the Conference spent some time on the main instrument to carry out the aims of the F L N, namely the Algerian Revolutionary Army. The Soumman Conference organized it into a regular army beginning with the rank of *djoundi*, the soldier, to that of the colonel who was in command of a *wilaya* (district). Political commissars were attached to each *wilaya*.

Recruitment to the A L N was voluntary although the F L N was in a position to call for a general conscription in many areas. The reports indicated that military manpower was never a problem to the A L N, for due to patriotism and political consciousness there were so many volunteers that many had to be turned away. The Algerian Muslim students had declared themselves under mobilization and offered to serve in the A L N. The aim of the A L N was to train the partisans in revolutionary warfare. Within its ranks there were workers, peasants, and intellectuals, and training schools were set up not only for military training, but also for political education.

Although the A L N constituted itself into a regular army, because its military strategy was that of guerrilla warfare it relied heavily on the peoples' support in the rural areas, particularly the *moussabilines* and the *fidayines*. These in fact were soldiers without uniforms, and they played the same role as the people's militia. The *moussabilines* were partisans who were recruited locally and who operated locally. Their duties included the sabotage of communications, the cutting of telegraph poles, intelligence work, the transport of munitions and care of the wounded. They also acted as 'guides' as well as decoys for the enemy. The *fidayines* on the other hand, carried out guerrilla operations against police stations, barracks, and the gendarmerie. They further engaged in acts of sabotage, such as setting fire to public buildings. In addition, it was their function to liquidate traitors to the national cause.

The ALN with its close links with the moussabilines and fidayines showed that what Algerian revolutionaries had in mind was not a war along conventional lines but a people's war against French colonialism. In this respect, the Algerian revolution was the first national movement on the African continent to adopt this form of struggle to achieve political independence.

There have of course been many armed uprisings amongst the peoples of Africa. In Madagascar in 1947, for example, such was the mass character of the insurrection that the French admit that they killed some 11,000 people. Another example is the peasant struggle for land in Kenya which engaged the British for several years, and which has come to be called the Mau-Mau movement. Likewise, there were armed struggles by peasants in areas of South Africa in the nineteen fifties. However, these were movements by the peasants, localized and often spontaneous, and their demands were specific rather than national.

For France the Soumman Conference was a double defeat. First, it was held right under the nose of the French in an area which they believed they had cleared of 'terrorists'. Secondly, the French were informed by their agents that it was the 'extremist' wing of the national movement which had taken control.

There is always a possibility that a colonially oppressed people, once they embark on an armed struggle to gain their freedom, will advance from the democractic phase to the socialist phase depending on which class is directing the struggle. In the case of Algeria, the F L N found that world imperialism supported France. On the other hand they found that not all socialist and communist countries and parties adopted the same position as the Communist Party of France. Some of the socialist countries were the strongest allies of the Algerian people. Not only did the F L N obtain arms from them, but also the benefit of the experience of such leaders as General Giap, the brilliant hero of Dien Bien Phu. A delegation from *El Moudjahid* visited North Vietnam and later published the report of an interview with Giap during which Giap spoke about the composition of the Vietnamese army.

> Our army is national, democratic and popular. It is national because it fights for the highest interests of the nation and for the independence of our people; democratic, because it includes within its ranks workers, peasants, intellectuals, people of all classes, belonging to all religions, who have a common ideal, and who are prepared to give the last drop of their blood for their country.
>
> I must also tell you that our army considers political education a decisive factor in the fighting ability of the soldier. It is only on the basis of well organized political work which continuously raises the national and revolutionary consciousness of the soldier that victories can be won.[3]

Earlier in the interview, Giap had said that the guerrilla relied on the people, served the people, and had their interests at heart. Even if freedom fighters were outnumbered and out-armed, victory would be theirs. Giap went on to say that the interests of the masses should always be paramount whether in victory or when the going was tough. The message was clear. The Algerian revolution had to rely on the people and always put their interests first. If this course was followed then victory was certain, and the revolution would move from the national democratic phase to socialist revolution.

The French government realized that it would not be

possible to contain the revolution by force of arms, and that sooner or later it would have to negotiate with the F L N. The crucial question was not so much the question of independence, but what would be the long term result? Would the granting of independence lead to the seizure of the commanding heights of the economy which France owned? Would independence mean the dismantling of all French military, air force and naval bases in Algeria? Would the new government allow France to exploit the oil-rich Sahara? In other words it became important that negotiations should be conducted with the section of the nationalist movement which would safeguard French interests. Ferhat Abbas was a man who could be relied upon to allow French economic interests to remain as well as its military bases. But Abbas had no real standing with the revolutionary leadership of the F L N.

For negotiations to succeed it was important to strike at the historic 'Nine'. Bitat had been arrested in February 1955. Then the French kidnapped foundation members of the F L N. This happened after the Soumman Conference, in October 1956. The kidnapped men were Ben Bella, Mohammed Khider, Hocime Ait Ahmed and Boudaif. However, the greatest blow the Algerian revolution suffered came with the capture of Ben M'Hidi in early 1954. He was brutally murdered. Not only was he a member of C N R A but a key member of the C C E in charge of general strategy. Mohammed Boulaif also died in the struggle. Belkacem Krim was the only one left of the 'Nine'. Bourgeois elements within the F L N were further strengthened because many of the militant leaders had been killed in the course of the fighting. One such leader was Amirouche. In addition, some of the outstanding organizers had been assassinated.

The Soumman Conference had not visualized the possibility of the C C E and the majority of the C N R A members leaving the soil of Algeria. But this is what happened. Outside the country, and deprived of direct contact with the masses some of them became victims of reactionary forces. This enabled the bourgeoisie to step in. The C C E membership was enlarged to nine and the C N R A to 54. This was contrary to the provisions of the Soumman Conference. Gone was the supremacy of the internal leadership over the external leadership. The C C E and C N R A decided to establish a Provisional Revolutionary Government of Algeria (G P R A). The composition of the G P R A was announced in September 1958. Ferhat Abbas was president. Belkacem Krim and Ben Bella were vice presidents. The G P R A, however, was the creation of C N R A which had been enlarged without the calling of a conference of both the exterior and interior leadership. The Soumman Conference of 1956 had been fully representative of all sections as well as of the A L N, and the internal sector had been recognized by all as being the supreme authority. The G P R A should have been formed as a result of a similarly representative conference. But it was established by leaders who were operating outside Algeria. To some extent the seeds of the future conflict were sown here because of the unrepresentative nature of the body. The failure to include within it the leadership of the A L N and the wilayas was fatal. Among the top leadership of the G P R A were men who had opposed the launching of the armed struggle. These men had only joined the F L N when it became apparent that it was likely to be victorious.

The G P R A became a battleground for two main factions, one led by Ferhat Abbas and the other by Belkacem Krim. In the power struggle the wings of Ferhat Abbas were clipped with the formation of the Interministerial Committee for Defence led by Belkacem Krim. After 1960 it was this Committee which held the real power. In 1961 Ferhat Abbas was replaced by Ben Khedda as President of the G P R A. The latter was a nominee of the Interministerial Committee for Defence. To the outside world the Ben Khedda government appeared more progressive than the previous one. The openly bourgeois wing had been eliminated. But on the most important political questions concerning the basis for negotiations with France, land reform, the political education of the people, a programme for the F L N, there was little difference between the two. Then Ben Khedda group stood for a neocolonialist solution which would protect French economic and military interests.

The G P R A having allotted portfolios to the leaders seemed more interested in concentrating its efforts in the diplomatic field. Here it scored some notable success. Arab countries such as Libya, Egypt and Lebanon recognized the G P R A. So also did China, North Vietnam, Mongolia and Yugoslavia. Ghana and Guinea were the first non-Arab African countries to recognize it. By 1960, some 19 countries had given de facto or de jure recognition.

In 1958 when the first Conference of Independent African States was held in Accra the question of armed struggle was raised and members discussed whether support should be given to a colonial people who had taken up arms for national independence. In attendance at the Accra Conference were Ghana as the host country, Libya, Ethiopia, Liberia, Morocco, Tunisia, Sudan and Egypt. The Conference side-stepped the question and passed the following resolutions:

The Conference of Independent African States
1. Recognizes the right of the Algerian people to independence and self-determination;
2. Deplores the grave extent of hostilities and bloodshed resulting from the continuance of the war in Algeria.

The Conference then urged France to enter into immediate negotiations with the Algerian Liberation Front to reach a fair and just settlement. It was clear that radical members of the Conference, like Nkrumah, were in a minority.

The attitude of the Conference did not satisfy the members of the Algerian Provisional Government which was composed of members of the F L N. Nkrumah, however, called another conference the same year, the All-African Peoples' Conference. This consisted of over three hundred delegates from all parts of Africa, representing African national movements. Here the issue of armed struggle was again raised. This time the majority of Conference members were in favour of the stand taken by the Algerian revolutionaries. Section 10 of the resolution on colonialism and imperialism stated: 'That the All-African Peoples' Conference in Accra declares its full support to all fighters for freedom in Africa, to all those who resort to peaceful means of non-violence and civil disobedience as well as to all those who are compelled to retaliate against violence to attain national independence and freedom for the people. Where such retaliation becomes necessary, the Conference condemns all legislations which consider those who fight for their independence and freedom as ordinary criminals.' In other words, the right of the oppressed to use violence as a reply to the violence of the oppressor was recognized.

The Tunis All-African Peoples' Conference, held in January 1960, went further.

General Resolution

The Second Conference of African Peoples assembled at Tunis from 25 to 30 January 1960, confirming the declarations and resolutions adopted at the first conference of African peoples held at Accra in December 1958:

Salutes the heroic people of Africa struggling for liberty, dignity and independence;

Bows before the martyrs fallen in the course of the glorious struggle against the forces of slavery and colonialist oppression; . . .

The Conference

. . . Recommends therefore the speedy setting up of an organization designed to co-ordinate the aid and solidarity of all the independent countries with regard to helping African peoples engaged in the struggle, and in particular the sending, at the request of the G P R A, of African volunteers to Algeria, the collection of funds and African information.

The resolutions on Algeria, therefore, were clear and unequivocal. The Conference saluted the progress made by the Algerian people in the war of independence under the direction of the FLN and the GPRA and paid special tribute to the combatants of the ALN. The result was that when the Conference of Independent African States met in Addis Ababa in June 1960, it came out in favour of the armed struggle of the Algerian people and called on all African governments to give material and diplomatic support.

Thus it can be seen that it was the Algerian revolution which struck the first blow against the road of non-violent struggle in Africa. Countries which had achieved independence through constitutional non-violent struggle, now supported the right of an oppressed people to wage armed struggle. It was from then onwards that imperialism stepped up its propaganda and tried to drive a wedge between the Arabs of the north and the rest of Africa, by saying that the Maghreb countries and Egypt were not really part of Africa. The real fear was that this method of armed struggle would spread to the rest of Africa still under colonial rule.

Revolutionaries are not against legal and constitutional struggles. The form of struggle, whether legal or illegal, non-violent or violent, will depend on the circumstances of a particular case. The considerations to be taken into account in each phase are the relative strength and weakness of the rulers as well as the fighting mood of the masses. In Vietnam, for example, the struggle passed through various phases. At a certain stage the attention was focused on the mobilization of the masses politically, and at the right moment an armed insurrection call was made in 1945. The guiding criterion in each phase is which method of struggle will most advance the cause of workers and peasants? If armed struggle becomes the principal method, it does not exclude other methods in specific localities and at certain times. Non-violence can be successfully employed as a tactic in the revolutionary struggle when it is considered likely to bring the required result. It is only when non-violence is adopted as an absolute principle that it becomes restrictive, and usually ends in victory for the oppressor. In the non-violent struggle it is the oppressed workers and peasants who sacrifice both their lives and their jobs. But the fruits of independence are snatched away from them by the bourgeoisie. The significance of the struggle in Algeria lay in that the masses were armed, and they distinguished themselves. Under such conditions, although it was still possible, it nevertheless would be difficult for the bourgeoisie to snatch all the spoils for itself after independence.

As far as Fanon was concerned, he held the view that the oppressed had the right to use force against their oppressors. In other words, the colonial peoples have the right to engage in armed struggle against imperialism for national liberation. Fanon devoted the whole first section of his book, *The Wretched of the Earth,* to the question of violence, and again and again stresses this point. 'Colonialism is not a thinking machine, nor a body endowed with reasoning faculties. It is violence in its natural state, and it will only yield when confronted with greater violence.'[4]

Fanon's exaggerations, his loose formulations or his mechanical approach, have laid him open to criticism. However, this does not invalidate his central theme that the oppressed have the right to use armed struggle to achieve their emancipation. Fanon was a member of the Algerian Provisional Government's delegation at the Accra All-African Peoples' Conference in December 1958, and helped to get the national movements to accept the principle of armed struggle.

6
ARMED STRUGGLE AND THE ACCRA ALL-AFRICAN PEOPLE'S CONFERENCE, 1958

Freedom is not a commodity which is 'given' to the enslaved upon demand. It is a precious reward, the shining trophy of struggle and sacrifice.[1]

PEOPLE who take up arms in order to win their freedom are under no illusions. They know it will mean suffering and sacrifice. But they also know that it will end suffering, if not for them, at least for future generations. Fanon, in his book *The Wretched of the Earth*, declares that the people 'record the huge gaps made in their ranks as a sort of necessary evil. Since they have decided to reply by violence, they are therefore ready to take all its consequences'.[2] Fanon held the view that independence and genuine decolonization could only be achieved as a result of violence. For freedom is never willingly granted to an oppressed people. It has to be seized from the oppressor. Kwame Nkrumah expressed much the same view when he wrote: 'I know of no case where self-government has been handed to a colonial and oppressed people on a silver platter. The dynamic has had to come from the people themselves'.[3]

It has been said that a revolution is the university for the masses. Within a few weeks they learn lessons which they would not be able to absorb in years. Though an exaggeration, Fanon made the same point when he wrote: 'Violence alone, violence committed by the people, violence organized and educated by its leaders, makes it possible for the masses to understand social truths and gives the key to them'.[4] Political consciousness certainly grows in the process of struggle. At the beginning, when the rulers state: ' "All natives are the same", the colonized person replies "All settlers are the same" '.[5] However, classifying all whites as oppressors does not last long. Fanon shows how, with the growth of political consciousness, the people begin to make a distinction between the white man and the oppressor. When fighting begins no prisoners are taken. But as the struggle continues and political education proceeds, the people differentiate between those who support the colonial power and those who are disgusted by the war.

The ultimate success of any struggle, according to Fanon, depends on the leadership's ability to unify the people and, in this task, it is not only political education, but armed struggle which can count. In fact, it is armed struggle which usually has the greatest unifying effect on colonized people. 'The practice of violence binds them together as a whole, since each individual forms a violent link in the great chain . . . The groups recognize each other and the future nation is already indivisible. The armed struggle mobilizes the people; that is to say, it throws them in one way and in one direction. The mobilization of the masses, when it arises out of the war of liberation, introduces into each man's consciousness the ideas of a common cause, of a national destiny and of a collective, history.'[6]

But if armed struggle unites, it also separates. Allies are united, and at the same time friend is clearly separated from foe. The enemies of the struggle who fostered division through tribalism or regionalism are on the other side of the barricades for all to see.

Fanon's training in existentialism, which lays heavy emphasis on the individual and his problems, shows when he adds: 'At the level of individuals, violence is a cleansing force. It frees the native from his inferiority complex and from his despair and inaction; it makes him fearless and restores his self respect.'[7] A people engaged in armed struggle do cast aside their slave mentality and get rid of many myths and superstitions which rob them of their confidence. But to take this down to the level of the individual is taking things too far. A national struggle has its heroes as well as its cowards. Violence can ennoble and make men more humane, just as it can degrade and brutalize. In such struggles ideology is important. Do the individuals believe that they are fighting a just cause? Do they hold freedom and independence more important than their own lives? If so, such men will make brave and fearless fighters. On the other hand, soldiers of liberation movements who have no clear understanding of the revolutionary struggle are easily defeated and demoralized.

For the sake of effect, Fanon at times becomes mechanical, and in the process is compelled to jettison truth. Thus he says: 'The reign of violence will be the more terrible in proportion to the size of the implantation from the mother country. The development of violence among the colonized people will be proportionate to the violence exercised by the threatened colonial regime.'[8]

In an armed struggle which gives scope for the worker and peasant to reveal his talents and ability, it is the intellectual who presents a problem. While the intellectual himself might have played a major role in the formation of the national movement, he hesitates to cast his lot with it when it takes the road of armed struggle. It is not that he is necessarily opposed to the struggle, but he lacks faith in the people and their ability to succeed. But at a certain stage many intellectuals do identify themselves with the struggle and this has the effect of turning them into new men. The struggle has become their spiritual bath which cleans away the dirt and filth acquired under colonialism.

Some of the important points that Fanon raises in his essay on violence are neither new nor original. His merit however lies in that he put them at a time when ideas of non-violent struggle had become fashionable and had gripped the minds of even radical intellectuals. His essay on violence thus challenges the ideas of non-violence and the latter's validity in Africa. In doing so he bent the rod a little too much on the opposite side. He exaggerates here, and makes a sweeping generalization there. But this is understandable, and he can be forgiven. The fact is that non-violent struggle had infected leaders of communist parties in Africa. Thus while they praised Lenin, Mao, and Ho Chi Minh for engaging in armed struggle, many felt that the time was not ripe for it in Africa, and the people were not ready for it. In the meantime they had donned the caps of Gandhi and had become 'passive resisters'. Some of them held a red flag with their left hand and a Gandhi cap with the right. Fanon's essay was directed not only against imperialists, but also against these 'communists' who had strayed from the path and who had taken the road of reformism. To the latter Fanon was their conscience, for he reminded them of what they should be doing.

It is difficult to assess the precise effect of Fanon's thought and his writings on the Algerian Revolution, and on opinion in France and the rest of the world. His articles in *El Moudjahid*, specially those which contained strong attacks on French colonialism and on the attitude of the French left and the Communist Party towards the Algerian struggle, were widely read at the time and have since been closely studied. Irene Gendzier in *Frantz Fanon, A critical study*, maintains that his criticism of the French left offended 'both Frenchmen and some of his colleagues on *El Moudjahid* who thought that he went too far'.[9] But there was doubtless no disagreement with his condemnation of those who advocated a peaceful and gradual approach to Algeria's economic problems. For Fanon as a staunch member of the F L N was committed to the armed struggle to end French colonial rule in Algeria.

In his articles in *El Moudjahid* and in his books, Fanon wrote of the problems of national liberation movements, of the Cold War and its effect on the peoples of the so-called Third World, of the dangers of neocolonialism, and of most of the other problems and difficulties facing peoples emerging from centuries of oppression. He was a master of political diagnosis but was less effective when prescribing a cure. However, his pan-African and international outlook succeeded in projecting the Algerian struggle not as a local rebellion but as a revolution. It was not surprising that although he was not an Algerian Fanon was quickly recognized by the F L N as one of their foremost militants.

On the formation of the G P R A in September 1958, Fanon worked for the Ministry of Information. The same year he was chosen as a member of the delegation to attend the historic All-African Peoples' Conference summoned by Kwame Nkrumah to meet in Accra in December 1958.

The gathering in Accra was the first of its kind ever to be held. Invitations had been sent out to leaders of national movements, like Jomo Kenyatta, Julius Nyerere, Hastings

Banda, Kenneth Kaunda and Patrice Lumumba. These headed national movements engaged in constitutional struggles to achieve independence, and they were soon to become heads of governments. But in attendance were also delegates from Angola, Guinea Bissau, Mozambique, and other areas still subject to white minority rule. Also present was Felix Moumié, leader of the Union of the Peoples of the Camerouns (U P A). These were to launch armed struggles in the future.

Kwame Nkrumah, the convener of the Conference of 1958, gave the reason for calling it in his book *Challenge of the Congo*: 'In spite of the national enthusiasm everywhere, there was no planning and directing centre to co-ordinate these movements for all Africa. Centres of the liberation struggle were set up in each territory with very little effective co-ordination between them . . . during the period 1945–1958 the African Revolution had no strategy.'[10] Giving the assault against imperialism an all-African character, he invited representatives from freedom movements from so-called British, French, Belgian, Portuguese and Spanish territories. In his own words: 'What I had in mind was to give the forces of the liberation movement the strategy to move into action and the tactics for that strategy . . . My object again was to infuse into the African Revolution new spirit and a new dynamism; and to create these where they were lacking.'[11]

It was the Algerian revolution that had the new spirit and dynamism which Nkrumah was seeking. It had gone from words to action. It did not expect imperialism to hand over freedom on a plate, but took the method of seizing it from the oppressor. On the two major issues, that of armed struggle and that of waging a continental struggle, the Algerian delegation to the Conference saw eye to eye with Nkrumah.

Fanon was pleasantly surprised that the Algerian delegation was accorded such a place of honour at the Conference. He wrote: 'We have discovered in Accra that the great figures of the Algerian Revolution – Ben Bella, Ben M'hidi and Djamila Bouhired – have become a part of the epic of Africa.'[12] Fanon noted that Kwame Nkrumah made a point of receiving the G P R A delegation among the first. For over an hour the Algerian problem was studied in relation to the liberation of the entire continent of Africa. Nkrumah pledged the support and the active solidarity of the people of Ghana to the fighting people of Algeria.

Enthusiasm for the Algerian revolution was not just verbal. F L N delegates became members of many committees, and one of the F L N delegates was elected to the Steering Committee. At the end of the Conference, Boumendjel, head of the Algerian delegation, was elected on to the Executive Committee of the All-African Peoples' Conference. On the other hand, as Fanon was quick to note: 'The few delegates who came to represent these puppet governments of French Africa found themselves more or less expelled from the commissions'.[13]

Although the majority of the delegates at the Conference were from national movements engaged in constitutional struggle, the Algerian delegates made no apology about the strategy of their struggle. They presented the problem of the armed struggle very clearly to the Conference. However, certain observers and journalists at first reported that Algeria had decided to adopt peaceful methods of struggle. But as the Conference got under way it became clear to all that the Algerian liberation movement was, 'a continuous, sustained action, constantly being reinforced, which contains in its development, the collapse and the death of French colonialism in Africa'.[14]

The Algerian delegation looked at this Peoples' Conference as one which also brought together the political, and the trade union organizations of the African continent. Their bond of unity was 'a national will opposed to foreign domination; their tactic, to weaken the colonizers one after another; their strategy, to frustrate the oppressor's manoeuvres and attempts at camouflage'.[15] *El Moudjahid* published a summary of the speeches of the three Algerian delegates. These were by A. Boumendjel, *On the struggle of the people of Algeria*; Mousteffai, on the *Liberation of*

Africa and Fanon on *Unity of the African countries*. It also gave a summary of Nkrumah's speech on continental unity. In his inaugural address Nkrumah said: 'We have nothing to lose but our chains and we have an immense continent to win'.[16] On the question of 'Africa for the Africans', a slogan raised at the Conference, Nkrumah, who never had any time for racialism, remarked: 'The concept – "Africa for the Africans" – does not mean that other races are excluded from it. No. It only means that Africans, who naturally are in the majority in Africa, shall and must govern themselves in their own countries.'

The presence of the Algerian delegation, its seriousness, its lucid analysis of the anti-colonial struggle, gave the Conference the dynamism and also the strategy that could be followed by national movements if rulers proved stubborn. In the words of Fanon: 'The Algerian war has in fact had a decisive bearing on this Congress. For the first time, it was realized, a colonialism, waging war in Africa proves itself powerless to win.'[17] It was because they had failed to analyse this phenomenon that colonialists were caught off guard and surprised at the success of the G P R A delegation. In endorsing the Algerian strategy, the Conference not only reaffirmed the right of the Algerian people to independence, but also recognized that the Algerians, and other oppressed peoples, had the right to retaliate violently when faced with the violence of the oppressor. 'The All-African Peoples' Conference in Accra declares its full support to all fighters for freedom in Africa, to all those who resort to peaceful means of non-violence and civil disobedience as well as to all those who are compelled to retaliate against violence to attain national independence and freedom for the people.'[18] *El Moudjahid* recorded that 'In the settlement of colonies of the type of Kenya, Algeria and South Africa there is unanimity: only armed struggle will bring about the defeat of the occupying nation'.[19]

Armed struggle broke out in Mozambique, Angola, Guinea Bissau, Zimbabwe, Namibia, and elsewhere. In South Africa, all the three national liberation movements, the Unity Movement of South Africa, the African National

Congress (A N C), and the Pan Africanist Congress (P A C), have accepted the principle of armed struggle. These have followed the new and dynamic strategy laid down at the Accra Conference. Nkrumah lived to see vast areas in the Portuguese colonies liberated by way of guerrilla warfare, and the opening up of many other guerrilla fronts.

On the question of continental unification, the G P R A delegation again saw eye to eye with Nkrumah. The fact that *El Moudjahid* emphasized this aspect of Nkrumah's speech showed that the delegation accepted his thesis. The delegation was enthusiastic over the idea of translating Pan-Africanism into practical terms by the creation of a continental force to liberate Africa from colonialism. Thus Fanon said : 'The African legion, the principle of which was adopted in Accra, is the concrete response of the African peoples to the will to colonial domination of the Europeans. In deciding to create a corps of volunteers in all the territories the African peoples mean clearly to manifest their solidarity with one another, thus expressing the realization that national liberation is linked to the liberation of the continent.'[18]

In spite of Nkrumah's repeated attempts over many years to get an All-African High Command set up, controlled and led by an All-African political party, this has not been done. And the resolutions passed at the Accra Conference have not been implemented, though they continue to be talked about and debated at most of the conferences and meetings held in Africa between governments, and organizations such as the O A U. At the same time criticism is voiced at the slow pace of decolonization, and attention is drawn to the aggression of neocolonialism and imperialism. But the root cause of the non-implementation of the Accra resolutions is the fact that many of the African puppet governments have more to lose than their chains. With the complete liberation of the African continent, and unification, they stand to lose their masters to whom they owe their positions. Some of the leaders fear their own masses more than they fear imperialism. Since the 1958 Conference there has been one qualitative change on the

African scene, and that is the realization that class struggle has broken out, and is raging side by side with the struggle of national movements fighting white minority regimes.

Fanon's first contact with Nkrumah, in Accra in 1958, had the effect of making him more aware of this phenomenon, and the dangers of the link up between the indigenous bourgeoisie and the international bourgeoisie. The true dimension of the African Revolution of which the struggle of the F L N formed a very important part, became clearer, and strengthened Fanon's belief that armed force was an essential method to be employed in the overall strategy of the Revolution.

In retrospect it may be said that the Accra All-African Peoples' Conference was one of the high water marks of the national phase of the African Revolution. When the next All-African Peoples' Conference takes place it is to be hoped that it will be a conference of socialist revolutionaries.

7
FANON AND THE NATIONAL BOURGEOISIE

The national bourgeoisie turns its back more and more on the interior and on the real facts of its underdeveloped country, and tends to look towards the former mother country and the foreign capitalists who count on its obliging compliance.[1]

THE problems faced by the F L N in the struggle to end colonial rule have, with varying emphasis, arisen in the course of most of the national liberation movements which have emerged throughout Asia, Africa and Latin America. Among them are problems of organization, leadership, ideology, tactics and strategy, and of base areas and supplies. Writing for *El Moudhajid* and working to get arms through to the F L N, Fanon was in a good position to experience such problems at first hand, and he has therefore some valuable assessments to contribute.

On the question of leadership and organization, Fanon came quickly up against problems posed by the role of the national bourgeoisie. The problem was not a new one. Marx and Engels, authors of the Communist Manifesto, described the bourgeoisie as a class of capitalists who were owners of the means of production and employers of wage labour. They saw the bourgeoisie as a product of a long course of development, of a series of revolutions in the modes of production and exchange. They noted that where the bourgeoisie was most developed, as in western Europe, there grew up also the petty bourgeoisie. This group was sandwiched between the bourgeoisie and the proletariat. It consisted of small scale manufacturers, landowning peasants, and businessmen. What distinguished them from the workers was the fact that they were owners of property, though it was on a small scale.

Lenin accepted the fundamental analysis of the bourgeoisie of Marx and Engels. But in the twentieth century, it became increasingly evident that the bourgeoisie could no longer thoroughly destroy feudalism and tribalism, or expand productive forces sufficiently. That historic role now fell on the working class.

Mao Tse-Tung, for his part, divided the bourgeoisie into three categories. There was the comprador bourgeoisie. In its original sense 'comprador' meant a Chinese manager, or senior Chinese employee in a foreign commercial establishment. As the class developed and grew in strength, even engaging in production, it nevertheless retained this characteristic, namely its ties and dependence on imperialism. The Chinese compradors were the big bankers, and those engaged in the export and import trade. Their ties with imperialism could be seen in their economic role in society. The second section was the national bourgeoisie, which owned the means of production, but these were not large employers of labour. Their opposition to imperialism was due to the fact that they had to compete against them in the exploitation of the Chinese working class. Meanwhile, they also feared the workers and peasants. There the political position of the national bourgeoisie was one of vacillation between imperialism and the proletariat. Its slogan was: 'raise your left fist to knock down imperialism, and your right to knock down the communists'.

In the third category, that of the petty bourgeoisie, Mao included middle peasants, handicraftsmen, lower levels of intellectuals, students, primary school teachers, lower functionaries, office clerks, lawyers and small traders. The petty bourgeoisie he divided into three sections. Politically, there was a small section which wanted to climb into the ranks of the bourgeoisie, and which veered to the right. At the other end of the scale, there was a section whose standard of living had fallen and which was joining the revolutionary proletariat. In between the two, there was a big layer which was neutral.

This analysis shows that the bourgeoisie in a semi-colonial country is not homogeneous and that there are fundamental contradictions within it. The conclusion that could be drawn is that not only would a section join the revolution, but that a big layer, normally neutral, might also be expected to lean towards the revolution. At the same time the vacillation of the petty bourgeoisie, its facing both towards imperialism and the working class, was recognized.

Fanon in his *Wretched of the Earth* sees the national bourgeoisie as a middle class without any economic power.

The urbanized elements which compose this group are doctors, barristers, traders, commercial travellers, and general agents, for this is the bourgeoisie which 'steps into the shoes of the former European settlement'.[2] In the rural areas it is the big farmers. In another part of the book he says that the top civil servants also form part of this group. In other words, his national bourgeoisie consists of the commercial, professional, bureaucratic and landed sections.

This bourgeoisie – and this is the basic fact – lacks economic power, because it is in general engaged in the services and not the productive sector. Fanon notes, although he does not elaborate, that the capitalist bourgeoisie is wholly absent for financiers and industrial magnates are not found within this national middle class. In general, the national bourgeoisie of under-developed countries are not engaged in production. Fanon condemns the national bourgeoisie for putting its own selfish interests before that of the nation, and for wasting the nation's assets. 'Since, moreover, it is preoccupied with filling its pockets as rapidly as possible but also as prosaically as possible, the country sinks all the more deeply into stagnation.'[3]

Continuing his analysis of the bourgeoisie in a chapter entitled *The Pitfalls of National Consciousness*, Fanon describes the role of the bureaucratic bourgeoisie. In a colonial economy, this intermediary sector is by far the most important. At independence, it is vital to bring the bureaucracy firmly under the control of the new government as quickly as possible. Where this had not been done, civil servants had established virtually a bureaucratic dictatorship. Fanon warned against apolitical civil servants. Those who lacked political education followed in the footsteps of their former colonial masters, and showed themselves incapable of acting in the interests of the nation as a whole. They sabotaged the national economy by indulging in all manner of selfish and corrupt practices.

The strength of the national bourgeoisie is based on its close links with international finance capital. Kwame Nkrumah has written about this alliance in his book *Class*

Struggle in Africa, and has shown that the basic interest of the African bourgeoisie lies in 'preserving social and economic structures'.[4] He went on to say that although 'the African bourgeoisie is small numerically, and lacks the financial and political strength of its counterparts in the highly industrialized countries, it gives the illusion of being economically strong because of its close tie up with foreign finance capital and business interests'.[5] Fanon did not analyse this important relationship between the national bourgeoisie and foreign finance capital though he did show that the national bourgeoisie in fact maintained most of the old colonial relationships: 'The national economy of the period of independence is not set on a new footing. It is still concerned with the ground-nut harvest, with the cocoa crop and the olive yield. In the same way there is no change in the marketing of basic products, and not a single industry is set up in the country. We go on sending out raw materials; we go on being Europe's small farmers who specialize in unfinished products.'[6] Fanon could well have been reporting about the Santiago U N C T A D Conference of 1972, for the position had not significantly changed.

The rural bourgeoisie also demands its share of the spoils which bureaucrats extract from the labour of workers and peasants. It is able to succeed with comparative ease because the bureaucrat, businessman or professional of the towns is very often also a landed proprietor. Fanon noted that at independence many big farmers demanded the nationalization of agricultural production. In many cases, they managed to take over all farms owned by settlers. But as the new landlords they seldom introduced any significant change in agricultural methods, or integrated their farming systems into a genuinely national economy. Very often, the new proprietors demanded more facilities and privileges than were enjoyed by the previous owners. Since this is the only section of the national bourgeoisie engaged directly in production, Fanon considered its members in practice no different from the previous exploiters. He remarked that on the take-over the exploitation of agricultural workers is intensified and made legitimate.

In his analysis of the national bourgeoisie, Fanon may be compared with Nkrumah, since both are concerned in their writings primarily with the national bourgeoisie which emerges after political independence. Nkrumah described it as parasitic: 'The African businessman is, in general, not so much interested in developing industry as in seeking to enrich himself by speculation, black marketeering, corruption and the receipt of commissions from contracts, and by various financial manipulations connected with the receipt of so-called "aid" '.[7] Nkrumah, in exposing its comprador nature, showed its dependence on the international bourgeoisie. But he did not see the African bourgeoisie as a homogeneous class. He saw various categories, and stated that the national bourgeoisie which emerged at independence was in reality a petty bourgeoisie. However, he recognized the revolutionary potentialities of some sections of the African bourgeoisie, 'Certain elements among the African bourgeoisie and traditional rulers – for example, revolutionary intellectuals – may dissociate themselves from their class origin and the ideology connected with it. These are "revolutionary outsiders", who can be absorbed into the ranks of the socialist revolution.'[8]

One of Nkrumah's most important contributions to the ideology of scientific socialism is his analysis of the bureaucratic bourgeoisie. These he listed as top civil servants, top men in the army, police, administration, and the party. 'The bureaucratic bourgeoisie, in particular, is the spoilt child of neocolonialist governments. Many African states spend ridiculously large sums of money on their bureaucrats.'[9] The reason why this section of the bourgeoisie is pampered is because of its close ties with foreign firms, usually the giant monopoly corporations who are given state contracts and liberal facilities to trade and invest.

It is clear that while there may be no developed capitalist bourgeoisie in Africa, there is nevertheless a bourgeoisie. Although economically they may be classified as petty bourgeoisie, yet they have political power and privileges associated with the bourgeoisie. The means of production in Africa, the factories, the mines and plantations are still largely owned by the international bourgeoisie. The national bourgeoisie is found mainly in the tertiary sector, that is, in the services sector of the economy. It is weak internally, and its strength really lies outside, in its connections with international finance capital.

Fanon did not make a detailed analysis of the various sections of the bourgeoisie, and as a result he was not able to see some of the contradictions amongst them. He was not able to appreciate that in the very process of capitalist development layers of the bourgeoisie were entering the ranks of the proletariat. In the time of Fanon, monopoly capitalism had already reached a stage where the monopolists of medium size in the older capitalist powers of Europe were being engulfed by the international monopolies. This became a common phenomenon in the decade of the sixties. The unevenness in capitalist development had the effect of creating instability. Ranks of the bourgeoisie were not only being forced into the proletariat by the process of capitalist development, but a section joined it for ideological reasons. The bourgeoisie cannot bring stability and order in their societies. Periodic monetary crises are an indication of their sickness. A section realize that only in a socialist society can there be any real stability and order. That is why there is a place in the struggle for those who break from their class to join the revolution.

The granting of political independence by the colonial powers was not an act of charity. It was in reality an act of give and take. The bourgeoisie, carefully groomed to take over, was expected to behave, and not to flirt with the socialist states. It was an unwritten agreement that their job in the whole set up was to see to it that profits and dividends were increased, and remitted regularly. In return, they were given the right to operate the state machinery, structured to facilitate the exploitation of the people. The imperialists also allowed them to accumulate a bit from this by way of commissions from the granting of state contracts.

In many of the colonies after independence, there were only two avenues of lucrative employment. First there was the state sector which Africanization opened up to the bourgeoisie. Secondly, there were jobs in the subsidiaries of the monopolies. It has become standard practice in neo-colonialist states for top civil servants, including cabinet ministers, to accept commissions when contracts are awarded. The 'honest man' is really one who accepts from only one side. So brazen have some become that they lay down a percentage for a contract to go through. In some cases they have bought farms from the departing colonialists and seen that aid from the government goes to these farms. Ministers, m.p's, permanent secretaries, are running businesses or have become slum landlords. In some parliaments there are m.p's who, in voicing the complaints of the people, say that top ministers and civil servants are seldom in government offices. They spend official time attending to their private farms or businesses. In this way the accumulation of private property is made possible through political and administrative power which a position in the state sector gives. Politics has become good business, and a job in the state sector 'pays'.

It is understandable why the struggle for state power assumes all the ferocity of the jungle. In Africa, to have state power is everything; without it, one is nothing. As in the jungle, the loser in the battle for state power is usually eliminated in one way or another. The proclamation of a single party state in a neocolonialist situation expresses the needs and aspirations of the national bourgeoisie. It does not want competitors, particularly from the working class.

Africa has had a rash of coups, many of them engineered by imperialism to prevent the masses from taking power when the indigenous bourgeoisie has failed to stop the march of the people. However, in some cases it has also been because of disputes among the bourgeoisie.

The national bourgeoisie is largely a petty bourgeoisie which controls and administers the machinery of state. In the country itself it has absolute political power even though it is dependent on imperialism. As the petty bourgeoisie then was subjected to the pressures of the two antagonistic classes so too now with the national bourgeoisie. On the one hand there is pressure from imperialism, while on the other hand there is pressure from workers and peasants and the socialist states. The result is that while the majority still retain strong links with imperialism, there are a few who are attempting to move out of the orbit of imperialism and to link up with the socialist states. In such cases the party leadership has responded to the desires of the people to break links with imperialism. But both wings of the national bourgeoisie have one thing in common, and that is their determination to have complete monopoly of political power in their hands.

Nkrumah called the national bourgeoisie 'a small, selfish, money-minded, reactionary minority amongst vast masses of exploited and oppressed people'.[10] Fanon saw it as senile, lacking in will, and timid. The national bourgeoisie which heads so many African governments has already become an anachronism. It is totally incapable of developing the productive forces in society for this would mean a confrontation with imperialism. It has developed as a subsidiary of imperialism, to act as a buffer between it and the masses. It has been placed in the driver's seat while the controls are being manipulated by imperialism.

8

CLASSES IN THE ALGERIAN REVOLUTION

It is clear that in the colonial countries the peasants alone are revolutionary, for they have nothing to lose and everything to gain.[1]

FANON'S observations on classes and class alliance have been criticized as shallow and misleading. He was not able to subject his impressions gained from first hand knowledge and experience to a rigorous scientific analysis. But it is not so much what he said about classes, but the fact that he turned the spotlight on to them that is important. He drew attention to the *fact* of class distinctions and class struggle in Africa at a time when it was fashionable to deny that classes existed in Africa. For class distinctions had become temporarily blurred as a result of the anti-colonial struggle, when there was a national front to achieve political independence. In addition, some intellectuals assumed hastily that, since the typical social structure within a colony was not instantly explicable in terms of the conventional Marxist scheme applied to the quite different European nations, classes and class forces did not exist.

In his book *The Wretched of the Earth*, Fanon mentions three major classes in African society, workers, peasants, and the national bourgeoisie. He also brings in two sub-classes, the intellectuals and the lumpen proletariat. In addition, he examines the feudalists, who are the big land-owners and chiefs. The purpose of his analysis is to decide which classes are revolutionary, and what is to be the nature of the revolution they seek to achieve.

Fanon correctly assessed the revolution in the colonies to be a national democratic one. Here he saw, though he did not elaborate, that this had two inseparable aspects, namely the national, which was for independence, and the democratic, which meant land for the peasantry. He was one of the few leaders at that time who emphasized the demand of the peasantry for land: 'The people . . . take their stand from the start on the broad and inclusive positions of *Bread and the land*: (his emphasis) how can we obtain the land, and bread to eat?'[2] The national democratic revolution therefore is aimed at achieving national independence, and is against feudalism, to satisfy the demand of the peasant for land.

A further question that has to be posed and answered is, who are the allies of the revolution? And what organizational form should the revolution take? The colonial peoples of the world have shown that the struggle is conducted through a national front, and this involves the unity of all oppressed classes. Since these classes have antagonistic interests, the question of leadership in the front becomes of cardinal importance.

Objective analysis will show that the most revolutionary elements in such a front will be the workers and peasants. The peasants constitute the majority of the population in a colonial country. They suffer from both feudal and capitalist exploitation. Like the urban workers, they too stand for a radical change in the status quo, and are a potentially revolutionary force. In some cases the peasantry is the driving force. The Vietnamese describe it as such, and say that the correct political line for revolutionaries is to base the front on a worker-peasant alliance. On the basis of this alliance it would be possible to rally the entire oppressed people and all the oppressed classes, including the national bourgeoisie and the section of enlightened feudalists. Such a front would also unite the various national minorities as well as religious groups.

The call for unity, based on worker-peasant alliance, flows from an objective analysis of the role of the classes. However, the actual position taken at the various stages of the revolutionary struggle will depend on a number of factors. At the best of times it will not be possible to rally the entire class. It will be sufficient if it is possible to rally a significant section. Factors to be considered in each case will be the degree of political mobilization, the past history of rebellion, past victories or defeats. Other questions would be whether trust has been established between, for example, the intellectuals and the peasants. Sometimes the rulers succeed in exploiting ethnic, religious and cultural differences so that temporarily a particular group may be on the other side of the struggle. Therefore, it is vital to know that not only are there sub-divisions within classes but that each class has its politically-conscious and politically-backward sections.

Fanon saw antagonistic contradictions between workers, while in fact there was fundamental unity. He remarks that it was a great mistake to approach in the first place the most politically-conscious in the towns, the skilled workers and civil servants. For although the proletariat has read the party publications and understands the nature of the struggle, it is much less ready to obey in the event of orders being given which set in motion the fierce struggle for national liberation. It refuses, according to Fanon, because it is privileged and pampered. Fanon is thus telling the nation and the peasants in particular, that the working class is undisciplined.

His views cause further unnecessary division between urban and rural workers when he says: 'The country people are suspicious of the townsman. The latter dresses like a European; he speaks the European's language, works with him, sometimes even lives in the same district; so he is considered by the peasants as a turncoat who has betrayed everything that goes to make up the national heritage. The townspeople are "traitors and knaves".'[3]

If the peasants are hostile, then the urbanized population, according to Fanon, show extreme distrust of the peasant: 'The overwhelming majority of nationalist parties show a deep distrust towards the people of the rural areas. The fact is that as a body these people appear to them to be bogged down in fruitless inertia. The members of the nationalist parties (town workers and intellectuals) pass the same unfavourable judgement on country districts as the settlers.'[4]

His views could cause further mischief and suspicion amongst the various members of the front when he deals with tribal chiefs and with intellectuals. He says that traditional chiefs are ignored and sometimes even persecuted. The intellectual he damns as a common opportunist. For Fanon believed that the intellectual, once he had cast his lot with the people, was afraid of being called a 'Yes-man' of the masses.

According to Fanon, the peasantry is the only revolutionary class, and the only sub-class which may be regarded as its revolutionary ally is a section of the lumpen proletariat. A better description of this section would be the 'peasant worker', or landless peasant: 'It is within this mass of humanity, this people of the shanty towns, at the core of the *lumpen-proletariat* that the rebellion will find its urban spearhead. For the *lumpen-proletariat*, that horde of starving men, uprooted from their tribe and from their clan, constitutes one of the most spontaneous and the most radically revolutionary forces of a colonized people.'[5]

Every revolutionary involved in the struggle for national liberation knows that in the course of the struggle, at some time or another, one can see some truth in Fanon's analysis of workers and peasants. Urbanized workers have been known to laugh at the dress and habits of migrant workers, and have passed remarks about them being 'uncivilized'. Likewise, one has met with peasants who distrust all strangers. But these opinions and views do not reflect the reality, in that they represent the views and opinions of politically-backward sections of people, whether they are workers, intellectuals or peasants. These are sections which have been afflicted with a colonial or slave mentality, and which are in need of political education. The task of the political organization is to eradicate such phenomena.

Fanon, despite what he has to say of the intellectuals, notes that in Algeria the revolution forged unity between the peasantry and a section of the intellectuals. For one of the greatest services that the Algerian revolution rendered the intellectuals of Algeria was to put them into contact with the people, by allowing them to see their poverty, and at the same time showing them their growing political awareness.

Workers and peasants are ready for revolutionary struggle, and have shown that they are ready to give their lives if necessary. However, they do need an organization with a leadership able to tell them from an objective analysis who their enemies are, and who their allies. It is the task of the leadership to weld the people into a national front and end colonial rule. In this sense, Fanon's analysis of classes is unhelpful, for it leads to a political cul-de-sac. In fact, any serious discussion on the unity of classes required in a national front to achieve independence, must either ignore Fanon, or begin with a criticism of his observations on this score.

A national front, whatever form it takes, is an organization that unites the three main classes in society because they have to fight a common enemy. These are workers, peasants, and the bourgeoisie to which the far-sighted section of feudalists also attach themselves. In such a unity, class relationships sometimes become blurred. But sooner or later, in the course of the struggle, particularly when it is an armed struggle, the crucial question arises as to who is to lead it?

In our historical epoch, there are only two classes who can discharge this historic task. The national liberation movement can only be led by the working class, or by the bourgeoisie. Even if the leadership positions may be held by the intermediate strata, the petty bourgeoisie, their political position is that of either the proletariat or the bourgeoisie. Therefore, who leads will determine the future course of the struggle.

In the case of the Vietnamese, the leadership of the national movement was in the hands of the party of the working class. Even if at the beginning of the struggle the slogans might not be far different from national movements led by the bourgeoisie, care was taken to ensure the supremacy of workers and peasants in the front. The national front in Vietnam consisted of peasants, workers, national bourgeoisie and landowners. However, the front was defined as one based on the peasant-worker alliance, led by the working class.

Radical elements of the M T L D constituted the foundation members of the F L N. In the course of the struggle the F L N opened its doors to all Algerians. It therefore became a front of workers, peasants, national bourgeoisie and feudal landowners. Every Algerian man or woman could become a member of the F L N. Later, this widened to include membership of an affiliated organization like the General Union of Algerian Workers (U G T A) and the General Union of Algerian Moslem Students (U G E M A).

When the F L N was formed, representatives of the bourgeoisie and the feudal landowners stood outside the struggle. They would have no truck with it because they saw in it a threat to their own positions and organizations. However, when the F L N caught the imagination of the people and became a mass movement, these elements from the propertied classes decided to change tactics, and to join the F L N. The F L N agreed to allow them to enter provided that they disbanded their organizations. At the time of the launching of armed struggle, there existed the Union Démocratique du Manifeste Algérien (U D M A) and the M T L D as well as the religious association of U L E M A. U D M A, U L E M A and the M T L D were reformist national movements, the leadership being in the hands of bourgeois and feudal elements. Although they talked of independence in front of the masses, they stood for collaboration with France. In other words, they wanted independence within the French Community. This would mean that while the national bourgeoisie controlled certain areas of administration in Algeria, the French government would retain powers over such sectors as defence and monetary matters. The reformist leaders even wanted French troops stationed in Algeria after independence. The organization of the priests, U L E M A, wanted the Arabization of schools, and some of them wanted an independent Algeria which would be a theocratic state.

The opportunist section of the bourgeoisie decided that instead of resisting the revolution it was better to join it and to capture the leadership. If they openly collaborated with the French then they would be finished in the eyes of the rapidly awakening Algerian people. The revolution had created a set of conditions where there could be no fence-sitting. One was either with the revolution or against it.

In Ferhat Abbas, the representatives of the Algerian

bourgeoisie and the feudal elements had an able spokesman. Unlike the founder members of the F L N he had been in the political struggle since the nineteen thirties. In the 'Bantustan' parliament which the French had set up before the war, he represented Moslem Algerians. In 1937 he belonged to the Union Populaire Algérie (U P A) standing for integration with France with equal rights for Moslems and French. The Algerian revolution did not change his stand. But he made a tactical shift. In 1954, Abbas was at the head of U D M A. He later dissolved it to join the F L N. U L E M A was also dissolved. Having complied with the conditions, Ferhat Abbas and other members of the bourgeoisie and feudalists were accepted into the F L N.

But Ferhat Abbas and his colleagues did not participate openly in the armed struggle. Instead, they joined the F L N outside Algeria when they fled to Cairo or Tunis. Thus while workers and peasants did the actual fighting inside Algeria, Ferhat Abbas and his clique plotted and schemed to gain control of the F L N.

The fact that the F L N was a mass, and not a cadre, party gave elements of the bourgeoisie ample room for manoeuvre. First, they changed their tactics. They became more 'revolutionary' than the real revolutionaries. In public places they made inflammatory speeches, and thus earned the title of being 'extremists'. Having donned the mantle of a revolutionary, Ferhat Abbas then visited socialist countries where his 'progressive views' were well received. This gave him the passport to enter into the ranks of the top F L N leadership.

There is little doubt that the founders of the F L N did not visualize an independent Algeria which would be a neo-colonialist state. Liberation was to end exploitation, at least feudal exploitation. Land reform would meet the aspirations of the peasants. Fanon put forward this aspect of the programme of the struggle when he said that from the very beginning the F L N defined its programme as aiming to end French occupation, to give land to the Algerians, and to establish a policy of social democracy in which men and women would have equal rights. What Fanon in fact was declaring was that the national movement should not narrow its demand to independence only, but should also incorporate the demand of the peasants for land. It was this demand for land for the Algerians, whether living as tenants, or as workers under French colons or Algerian landlords, which would give the Algerian national movement its democratic character.

The Algerian bourgeoisie did not attack the land programme of the F L N openly, but they kept putting off discussion of the issue until after independence. They emphasized in public that the people should put in every effort to win independence. In private, however, they urged that the struggle against feudalism be shelved as this might drive the landlords into the arms of the French.

The first attempt to capture the leadership of the F L N was at the Soumman Conference in 1956. The issue that was posed here was not one of programme or policy, but an apparently harmless one of, where the supreme political and military power should reside? Should it be with those inside Algeria who were engaged in actual combat, or with those who were in Cairo, Tunis or Morocco? In other words should supreme power reside in the internal or external leadership?

Unlike in Vietnam or in southern Africa where a leader has also to be a soldier, in Algeria, many leaders like Ferhat Abbas were civilians. The difference over leadership, whether external or internal, was in reality a struggle between the revolutionary wing and the conservative wing of the F L N. The Soumman Conference decided that the supreme authority for both political and military matters rested with the internal leadership. This then, was a victory for the trend leaning towards peasant and workers, for a leadership remaining on the battlefield itself would be more responsive to the pressure of the masses, the peasants, who were the chief combatants.

As long as the internal leadership remained in control, it was not possible for the bourgeoisie to seize the reins. It had to be content with building up its leaders in the eyes of the masses and in countries supporting the struggle. But eleven months after the Soumman Conference, there was an unexpected development when four of the internal leaders fled from Algeria. The bourgeoisie now saw its chance, and it struck. Therefore, when the supreme council met and enlarged itself, Ferhat Abbas took over the vital portfolio of Information, and in the diplomatic offensive this was a key portfolio. He was also in a position to decide what information should be broadcast to the Algerians.

Shortly afterwards, when the GPRA was formed, Ferhat Abbas became prime minister, and then it was clear that the bourgeoisie had taken over control. The GPRA was then the supreme authority and became the government in exile. In 1959 so strong did Ferhat Abbas feel about his position that in an interview he said, 'I prefer a French presence to a Russian or American presence. I speak French'. This was another way of telling the French bourgeoisie that its Algerian counterpart was ready to do a deal. De Gaulle, representing the aware section of French imperialism, realized that it would be better to negotiate with Ferhat Abbas than with an Algerian Ho Chi Minh a few years later. What was at issue behind whether independence was to be within the French Community or outside it, was how far was the GPRA prepared to preserve the economic and strategic interests of French imperialism? If there was a definite guarantee, de Gaulle was prepared to sacrifice the colons. The issue they had come to negotiate was whether independence was to be within the French Community or independence with 'secession'. But in either case it was understood that French vital interests would not be jeopardized.

Ferhat Abbas was able to worm his way up and to seize control of the FLN for three main reasons. First, some countries which gave material support to the Algerian revolution were bourgeois and feudal states. While they welcomed FLN militants, and housed them, they nevertheless were determined to see that the government of the Algeria which emerged after the revolution would not be radically different from their own governments. Tunisia, for instance, had been granted independence but had French troops stationed there to protect the new rulers. These governments favoured Abbas and his group of 'moderates'. Secondly, the method by which the bourgeoisie gained control of the F L N meant also that the external leadership had taken over from the internal. This was possible because of the absence of a politically-aware disciplined party, which would have been able to unify all the genuinely revolutionary sections. Thirdly, under conditions of guerrilla warfare a considerable degree of decentralization is essential. This gives the fighters scope for initiative and the ability to make quick decisions on the spot. But this reinforces the need for a strong centralized leadership operating within the territory. That being absent after the G P R A was set up, it was small wonder that regionalism developed, and some of the top commanders began to behave like feudal lords.

Many of the original leaders of the F L N were inside the territory, or had been killed. Others like Ben Bella had been kidnapped and were in prison. They were not, therefore, in a position to steer the policies of the F L N along revolutionary lines which would meet the aspirations of the masses. The cadres, imbued with nationalist ideology, were not able to stand up to the onslaught of the bourgeoisie, and to see through their camouflage.

The formation of the G P R A did not lead to an intensification of the struggle. The opposite was the case. The military aspect of the struggle was downgraded and it was the diplomatic fight which received first priority. Members of the external leadership saw themselves as future presidents, prime ministers, or holders of other high offices. Therefore there was a veritable scramble for positions in the 'shadow cabinet', and the struggle became a contest for control of the G P R A. The fight for leadership became primary, the continuation of the armed struggle secondary.

This internecine fight for positions caused havoc in the struggle inside Algeria. Fighters were continually short of the much needed arms, ammunition, food and medical supplies. There was a virtual absence of any type of political education of the cadres. So serious was the neglect that A L N commanders met and commissioned one of them, Amirouche, to get in touch with the external leadership to inform them of the perilous state of affairs. Amirouche did not deliver the message personally for he was killed in battle.

The struggle for power by different sections of the bourgeoisie eventually led to the overthrow of Ferhat Abbas as head of the G P R A. Ben Khedda took his place. He did not have the same background as Abbas and was reputed to be an 'extremist' who had been one of the founders of the F L N. But the French, in secret negotiations, found him equally acceptable for he had indicated that his provisional government was willing to lease military bases to France, to grant France land communications with Sahara States, and to co-operate in a joint exploration and exploitation of the Sahara. Rich oil and gas deposits had been discovered in the Sahara desert.

In some ways, Ben Khedda was even more acceptable to the French, for not only was he one of the founder members of the F L N but he had been elected in the Soumman Conference to be one of the five members of the Supreme Council. He had the reputation of being tough. De Gaulle shrewdly observed that Ben Khedda's policies seemed no different from those of Abbas. Ben Khedda was willing to guarantee French interests in both military and economic spheres for at least five years. Abbas had a past record which tended to make F L N militants suspicious of him. Therefore, the French preferred to negotiate with Ben Khedda since he was more acceptable to the F L N and was at the same time prepared to fulfil much the same role as Abbas. The result of the negotiations between France and the G P R A resulted in the Evian Agreement signed in March 1962. The following are the chief points of this Agreement:

Culture: While Algeria was to retain French cultural institutions, it was not bound to them indefinitely. Some radio broadcasts and texts were to be made available in French, and the European population would be able to conduct administrative business in French. The Algerian higher educational system with French aid would be modelled on the French system.

Economics: Algeria would remain in the franc zone, but was free to establish protective tariffs and to negotiate its own relations with the European Common Market. The Algerian government was to be allowed to nationalize land and property provided this was done without discrimination between Moslems and Europeans, and provided that compensation was paid. France was to contribute to the compensation of dispossessed Europeans. Capital could be withdrawn from Africa provided that the economy was not seriously harmed. French Sahara schemes would continue to operate with profits shared between the two countries. France would provide technical assistance, training and personnel to the best of her ability.

Military: French air bases in Algeria would be retained for five years and flights to them assured. The El Kebir naval base was leased by France for fifteen years.

Fanon did not live to witness the shameful betrayal of the revolution by the Algerian bourgeoisie. All the strictures he had written about the national bourgeoisie would have now been applicable to the Algerian counterparts. Their role was even more criminal because blood had been shed by peasants and workers, and the bourgeoisie was stepping in to snatch the fruits of their sacrifice. The betrayal lay precisely in the sphere of ending feudal relations in land and the failure to satisfy the aspirations of the peasantry which had borne the brunt of the fighting and suffering. It was clear that the Ben Khedda leadership was not going to carry out the agrarian revolution which is the basis of a national democratic programme. The only land which they would make available to the peasant was that which the colon had vacated and for which the French government would contribute compensation.

It is small wonder that the militants and radicals of the F L N rallied round Ben Bella, who found in Boumedienne a valuable ally. The Evian Agreement was one between the

Algerians and the French. But the people wanted to know just what type of society was to arise as a result of their heroic sacrifice and suffering. In greed and haste, sections of the bourgeoisie had forgotten the people. The Tripoli Programme in which Ben Bella had an important hand, defined the new goals of revolution as socialism, anti-imperialism, a society in which the commanding heights of the economy would be controlled by the people. The Tripoli Programme in fact repudiated the significant sections of the Evian Agreement. It is small wonder that the 1962 Agreement was denounced for giving special privileges to the colons, and for tying Algeria's culture and its economy to France. The Tripoli Programme particularly exposed the military link with France, which it characterized as part of neocolonialist strategy.

The Evian Agreement was an excellent example of 'independence within the French Community'. There was no change in the economic system, nor in the structure of the state machinery. The only change visualized was one of mastership, with the Algerian bourgeoisie and the feudal landlords replacing French imperialists and the colons.

The French and their junior partners in exploitation, the Algerian bourgeoisie, had ignored one factor. The people were armed. They had suffered over a million casualties and another two million people had been completely uprooted from their homes and villages. If all their sacrifices were not to be in vain, they too had to strike out and to put their stamp on the revolution. It was under Ben Bella-Boumedienne leadership that the masses struck at the bourgeoisie.

Fanon died before the end of the Algerian war. Had he lived, he may well have modified some of his more controversial views on classes and class alliance in the national liberation movement. As it was, he rendered the revolutionary struggle a valuable contribution by focusing attention on class struggle, and by exposing the opportunists and bourgeois elements who were attempting to betray the people and to sabotage the African Revolution.

9
FANON ON RACISM

The liberation of the Algerian national territory is a defeat for racism and for the exploitation of man.[1]

EVEN if workers and peasants in a national liberation movement are infected with racialism temporarily, it is not part of their ideology, nor does it objectively serve their interests. However, at a certain stage in the development of a national movement, racialism rears its ugly head and the most progressive sections of the leadership have to fight it. In its open manifestation it takes the form of identifying the oppressor with the colour of the skin. But with increased political awareness, members of the movement learn that the struggle is not against persons of a particular colour, but against oppression and exploitation. Exploiters and oppressors may be black, while those assisting the liberation movement may be white. The real friends and the real enemies of the revolution are recognizable through other criteria. The guiding factor is, what is the objective role of a person or a group? Do they by their words or actions advance the struggle or retard it? This criterion cuts across racial and colour lines. Individuals from white races have assisted the struggle, while those of the same colour of the masses of oppressed have turned traitors, and have consciously assisted the enemy.

However, from the recent experience of national movements, it has been shown in many cases that it is the petty bourgeoisie, the property-owning and privileged section in the national movements, which carries the racialism of the rulers and spreads it to the people after inverting it. What is essentially a struggle between the oppressor and the oppressed is turned into a struggle between white and black. What in reality is an anti-imperialist struggle, they see as a racial war. There are good and solid reasons for this. They aspire to step into the shoes of their masters. But to prevent an exposure of their ambition, they keep the political consciousness of the people at a very low level. Racialism therefore becomes a smokescreen to promote class interests.

Fanon came from an intellectual background which was

free from racialism. His association with Sartre in the formative period of his intellectual life and his marriage to Josie got rid of any traces he might have acquired during his earlier years. Yet in a series of articles appearing in *El Moudjahid* on 1, 15 and 30 December 1957 on French intellectuals he wrote: 'The status of the foreigner, of the conqueror, of the Frenchman in Algeria, is that of an oppressor. The Frenchman in Algeria cannot be neutral or innocent. Every Frenchman in Algeria oppresses, despises, dominates.'[2] He further asserted that every Frenchman in Algeria was an enemy soldier. Taken out of its context, Fanon seems to be accusing every Frenchman of being an oppressor, and every colon in Algeria of being an enemy. Such accusations could only fan the flames of racialism and cloud the basic political issue at stake. This does little justice to Fanon, and is inconsistent, for all his political life Fanon attacked racialism, whether it came from whites or blacks.

The real Fanon is revealed when he wrote an article in *Les Temps Modernes* in June 1959. In this he showed the contribution made by the Jewish minority, certain colons and urban Europeans to the Algerian liberation struggle. For indeed it would be rampant racialism to confuse the Zionist state of Israel with the Jewish people.

The Jews in Algeria represented about one-fifth of the non-Moslem population. Fanon correctly pointed out that their attitude to the revolution should not be regarded as a homogeneous one. There were classes among the Jews. The big Jewish businessmen, who were in league with the French administrators, regarded the Algerian businessmen as potential competitors. Therefore, to protect their economic interests they sided with the French. However, in certain rural areas, the small Jewish trader cast his lot with the revolution. 'Jewish tradesmen furnish the A L N its supplies of military clothes, blankets . . . It is no secret that since 1954 several Jewish tradesmen have been arrested for aiding and abetting the Algerian revolution.'[3]

Jews constituted a significant sector in the bureaucracy. This sector did not relish the idea of independence for they feared it would mean their own displacement. But Fanon pointed out that there were occasions when Jewish police officers prevented the arrest of patriots and even helped them to escape. This then was the other side of the coin. But in the case of the Jewish masses whom Fanon names the 'highly Arabised mass',[4] there was no problem, for they regarded themselves as Algerians. These Jews knew little French, and associated actively with the revolution.

The Jews, as a minority, came between the French rulers and the mass of the Algerian people. They thus had no effective power. Under French rule they were never secure, for racial prejudice manifested itself in anti-semitism. However, in relation to the Algerians, they were seen as having a social and economic position one or two pegs higher than that of the Algerians. A small section of the Jews were given preferential treatment in the civil service, and in the institutions of higher learning, as well as in trade. The aim was not to advance the Jews but to divide them from the rest of the Algerians. The Algerian worker and peasant, not understanding the complicated mechanisms of capitalism and how surplus labour is extracted, would look at the petty Jewish shopkeeper with whom he came into contact as the 'exploiter'.

In a sense, the Jewish barometer was the barometer of the revolution. Being sandwiched between both revolution and reaction it was subjected to pressure by each at the same time, or in turns. The F L N realized that the Jewish community in Algeria was not homogeneous and that it had class divisions. However, it felt that the majority of Jews were subjected to oppression and exploitation like the Algerians. At the Soumman Conference their position was discussed and analysed and a call was made to them to stop sitting on the fence and to take sides. The call read: 'Algerians of Jewish origin have not yet overcome their qualms of conscience, nor chosen sides. Let us hope they will, in great number, take the path of those who have responded to the call of the generous fatherland, and have given their friendship to the Revolution by already proudly proclaiming their Algerian nationality.'[5]

The far-sighted, politically-conscious section of the Jews had realized that they as a people had been in Algeria for over 2,000 years and that they were an integral part of the Algerian people. It was the policy of French imperialism to try to separate Jews from Muslims. But many Jews made common cause with the F L N. Within six months it could be said that, 'Jews have joined the ranks of the Algerians fighting for national independence . . . Some have paid with their lives, others have bravely borne the foulest police brutalities, and many are today behind the doors of prisons and the gates of concentration camps'.[6] Fanon showed his complete agreement when he wrote : 'Jewish lawyers and doctors who in the camps or in prison share the fate of millions of Algerians attest to the multi-racial reality of the Algerian nation'.[7] Had Fanon been a racialist, he could easily have given way to anti-semitism which was prevalent amongst the French rulers and amongst certain strata of the Algerian intelligentsia. On the contrary, Fanon made an honest and objective analysis and pointed out that their attitude to the revolution was not homogeneous.

The policy of the F L N was not to enrol Jews as combatants, even though they volunteered. But they were asked to become the eyes and ears of the revolution. They thus advised local revolutionary leaders of the size of French units, the nature of their arms, the routes to be followed, and the times of patrols. In addition, many Jews contributed financially in the struggle, and made monthly contributions through intermediaries.

Another myth attacked by Fanon, which again shows his non-racial approach, was the myth that *all* Algeria's settlers were opposed to the end of colonial rule. He pointed out that many French settlers had given support to the people's struggle : 'Even the Algerians have been surprised by the frequency with which the settlers have responded to the appeals of the F L N. In any case, once contacted by the F L N, no settler has ever reported to the French authorities. It has happened that they have refused an appeal, but the secret has always been kept.'[8] There were about one million settlers out of a population of ten million. Some of them had lived in Algeria for over three generations. It was not surprising, therefore, that when the revolution broke out many of them at once took sides. Fanon wrote that many farms belonging to European settlers had been used by the F L N as hospitals, refuges or broadcasting stations. When the French troops began to make a habit of systematically destroying the grain reserves of the Algerian population, the A L N decided to hide their supplies on European farms. Several farms belonging to Europeans were transformed into A L N granaries, and at night A L N units would descend from the mountains to collect supplies of wheat or semolina.

It was because colons participated in the revolution that many of them were arrested. Fanon said they were imprisoned for 'arms traffic, arms transport, financial support'.[9] It has been argued that some of them supported the F L N because they wanted to safeguard their own future, and that this help was a form of insurance policy against future expropriation. Whatever may have been the reason, and here one cannot go into motives, the objective role was to split the imperialist bloc in Algeria, to isolate the French colonizers and therefore to bring independence nearer.

The Algerians were fighting a just war and therefore they were able to rally to their side the politically-conscious from among the French population in Algeria. This was certainly the case with a certain strata of urban Europeans and intellectuals. Fanon, who confronted this section on many occasions and knew them well, described how European doctors, pharmacists and nurses began to treat wounded A L N members without discrimination. As the French repressive apparatus began to disintegrate, the Europeans became more audacious. They would carry arms through road blocks because they would not be suspected. A stage was reached when even the police would report to the local F L N cell when an operation was planned. They would warn an Algerian that he was being watched, or would advise him that a tortured prisoner had been made to talk and had named him as the local F L N chief.

Fanon, in paying tribute to the work of Jews and Europeans, named the example of Maitre Thuveny as a worthy example of one of the best representatives from among the whites who had joined the F L N. The most precious possession a man has is his life and Thuveny gave this for the cause of the revolution he held so dear. He was an attorney in Oran, and according to Fanon fought for a long time in the ranks of the F L N, and died as a result of an assault organized in Morocco by the French Second Bureau.

This outlook, cutting across racialism, has deeply influenced the national liberation movements fighting in southern Africa and elsewhere. In Mozambique, for example, Frelimo has successfully fought the erroneous tendency of looking at all people of other races as enemies. Other liberation movements are tackling the same prejudices. Samora Machel of Frelimo, in his message to the people of Mozambique on the eighth anniversary of the launching of armed struggle, proclaimed: 'The Mozambican people fraternally invite Portuguese soldiers and the Portuguese population to unite in the common endeavour for liberation.' Such a call would have delighted Fanon since it cuts right across racism and indicates that the liberation movement is on a sound ideological basis. For racism is a product of bourgeois thinking, and is not to be found among those who genuinely seek to end the oppression and exploitation of man by man.

10

THE ROLE OF WOMEN

Side by side with us, our sisters do their part in further breaking down the enemy system and in liquidating the old mystifications once and for all.[1]

FANON had left Blida Hospital and joined the F L N not only because he wanted to see the end of the oppressive colonial system, but also because he wished to see the emergence of a new society in Algeria. Even if he did not know exactly what kind of society this would be, he nevertheless envisaged that it would be modern, based on science and technology, and that it would be a society in which women would occupy an honourable place. He believed that in the process of armed struggle against French imperialism, the Algerian society's own myths, superstitions, and medieval relationships would also be swept away.

One of the tests of a real revolutionary in a colonial country is not only whether he stands up for the liberation of the oppressed, but whether he also supports the emancipation of women. For Fanon there was no personal problem on this score. He was very much concerned about the depressed position of women in African society. He did not analyse the problem from a historical point of view, and examine the monogamous family under capitalist society as a development from previous societies. He therefore did not connect their depressed position with the existence of private property. What he did do, however, was to show very vividly, the impact of the revolution on the Algerian family system, and how the requirements of the struggle set in motion the process of women's emancipation.

The advent of capitalist society gave women a measure of theoretical equality, but never completely emancipated them. The laws of a minor, where a woman could not be a party to a binding contract, applied generally until only recently. However, this did not prevent ideologists of the French bourgeoisie using the degraded position of women in Algerian society to cut them off from the Algerian intellectual, by despising them for their backwardness. These French intellectuals while remaining silent at the monstrous oppression of the colonialists attacked the Algerian man for turning his woman into an 'inert, domonetized, indeed dehumanized object'.[2]

During the time he was on the editorial board of *El Moudjahid*, Fanon dealt frequently with the question of the role of women in the revolution. In an article which appeared in May 1957 he wrote: 'In the Algerian family, the girl is always one notch behind the boy . . . The girl has no opportunity, all things considered, to develop her personality or to take any initiative. She takes her place in the vast network of domestic traditions of Algerian society. The woman's life in the home, made up of centuries-old customs, allows no innovation . . . The woman in an underdeveloped society, and particularly in Algeria, is always a minor, and the man – brother, uncle or husband – represents first of all a guardian . . . The facility with which divorce is obtained in Algerian society imposes upon the woman the weight of an almost obsessional fear of being sent back to her family.'[3] This then was her burden, her harassment, her insecurity before the revolution.

When armed struggle began, the F L N did not call upon women to take part in it. To fight was considered a male affair. But with the rapid growth of the struggle, the liberation movement had to contend with the enemy mobilizing all its human and natural resources. Press, radio, church, educational institutions, were harnessed by the French to wage the battle of annihilation. Faced with total war, the F L N soon understood that the fighting would be protracted and that it was not just a question of ambushes, sabotage or open battle any more. The war of liberation meant organizing finance, intelligence, political training. It involved caring for the wounded, as well as for the education of the young. In other words, the total mobilization of French imperialism could only be met and challenged by the total mobilization of the people. A guerrilla war had to be turned into a full-scale war. A national movement of liberation could then take the form not only of a war of men; but women must be mobilized and fully involved. A woman who was restricted and virtually imprisoned in her cloistered home was a liability. Only an emancipated woman would be able to withstand the terror and to rise to the tasks entrusted to her by the revolution. This meant that the veil had to go. An unveiled woman was a sure sign of emancipation.

The women of Algeria had to fight to cut through centuries of prejudice and taboos imposed on them by feudal, patriarchal society. Women eventually won their right to participate in the struggle for independence, and the process set in motion a movement for their own emancipation. Fanon described this process and showed how male resistance was slowly broken down: 'Until 1955, the combat was waged exclusively by the men. The revolutionary characteristics of this combat, the necessity for absolute secrecy, obliged the militant to keep his woman in absolute ignorance . . . The decision to involve women as active elements of the Algerian Revolution was not reached lightly . . . The women's entry into the war had to be harmonized with respect for the revolutionary nature of the war. In other words, the women had to show as much spirit of sacrifice as the men.'[4]

There was no need for such anxiety. A woman, like any oppressed and exploited person, once given a chance to unlock her creative talents, is capable of performing heroic and magnificent feats. In the struggle, a woman like her male counterpart is arrested, tortured and shot. As a woman she often suffers more, for sometimes she is raped by her captors. Taboos and prejudices broke down when married women militants were admitted to the F L N. Later, the door was opened for widows and divorcees. Soon, the rush to join the F L N from unmarried girls led to the removal of all restrictions and to the acceptance of all Algerian women.

Women nursed the wounded F L N. In villages where the men had vanished into the forests and mountains, women took over the jobs of being teachers of the youth who would later be the militants of the revolution. Once the veil was ripped off, women quickly mastered the art of underground work, and carried out important missions. Fanon wrote about one aspect of this work when he described them, 'carrying revolvers, grenades, hundreds of false identity cards or bombs, the unveiled Algerian woman moves like a fish in the Western waters. The soldiers, the French patrols, smile to her as she passes, compliments on her looks are heard here and there, but no one suspects that her suitcases contain the automatic pistols, which will presently mow down four or five members of one of the patrols'.[5] In another paragraph he said that she might be carrying in her bag or small suitcase, millions of francs belonging to the revolution, money to be used to take care of the needs of families of prisoners, or to buy medicine and supplies for the guerrillas.

The participation of women in the revolution boosted F L N membership. 'The female cells of the F L N received mass memberships. The impatience of these new recruits was so great that it often endangered the traditions of complete secrecy.'[6] Their involvement gave the movement its depth, strength and totality. But the participation of women in the revolution was double-edged. Their particular contribution to the Algerian revolution involved not only a struggle against French domination but also against male hegemony and social inequality. In this struggle the women had the support of the far-sighted section of the F L N. And in Fanon, the women had an enthusiastic champion for their cause.

One of the areas in which women challenged the old order was over marriage. Hitherto, it had been a prerogative of the patriarch to give away his daughter in marriage. The choice was more often made by the patriarch. The girl whose life was to be lived with another man had little say in the arrangement. But with the war, families were scattered and women lived a life free from the authority of parents or guardians. A woman now chose her future life partner and all the couple did was to approach the superior officer for permission to marry. Fanon noted that such unions were entirely voluntary: 'The future wife and husband had had time to know each other, to esteem, to love each other.'[7] The officer had no alternative but to give permission, and these marriages became so common in the liberated areas, that the authorities had to open up bureaux to register marriages, births and deaths.

In the liberated areas a wonderful tradition grew up which was to sweep the whole country. It began when a certain girl questioned the character and qualifications of her future husband. The girl refused to marry the boy because he was not a soldier in the army of liberation. In other words, the women were demanding an extra qualification in addition to honesty, education and thrift. Their suitor had to belong to the F L N and to be a fighter for the revolution. According to Fanon, the father's authority in the family was severely shaken by this new requirement.

Within a year, such was the work of the women that their dedication and heroism against tremendous odds led to the Soumman Conference discussing the possibility of granting them greater responsibility. The F L N leaders at this meeting recalled that since the French occupation of their country from 1830, wherever there was resistance or revolt, women had participated very actively. In particular, the leaders at Soumman recalled the rebellions in 1864 of Ouled Saidi and of Kabilya in 1871, and in the Aures region in 1916. In all these, women distinguished themselves through their heroism and unlimited capacity to suffer and to sacrifice. The Conference therefore took the opportunity of praising young girls and women for their courage and bravery. Alongside the *moudjahides* (men fighters) the *moudjahilibes* (sisters) were mentioned as those who had dedicated their lives for the liberation of the fatherland. Specifically, the Conference said that it was possible to organize them while at the same time observing the traditions of the people. Their new tasks were to be:

— to raise the morale of the combatants and fighters
— to gather intelligence, act as liaisons, to provide supplies, and to give shelter to the fighters
— to aid the families of soldiers who were imprisoned.

Fanon frequently paid tribute to the women of Algeria, saying that revolutionary activity had been carried out by women with exemplary constancy, self mastery and success.

'Revolutionary war is not a war of men . . . it is a total war in which the woman does not merely knit for or mourn the soldier. The Algerian woman is at the heart of the combat. Arrested, tortured, raped, shot down, she testifies to the violence of the occupier and to his inhumanity.'[8] She ceased 'to be a complement for man. *She literally forged a new place for herself by her sheer strength*'.[9] Her personality also blossomed as she discovered the exalting reality of responsibility. What it meant for the Algerian people as a whole was that it emancipated the Algerian man also, for the freedom of the Algerian people became identified with women's liberation.

Fanon realized that this was only the beginning, a few steps along the very long road. He knew that old customs, prejudices, handed down from time immemorial, could not be ended within a few years. He saw the struggle ahead. But for himself he was behind the women, and he urged and encouraged them to go ahead.

There was not the same enthusiasm to champion the cause of women's emancipation after independence had been achieved. The National Union of Algerian Women (U N F A) could not hold its first national congress until four years after independence. Some leading women militants went back to wearing the veil after marriage. One woman presented a sorry picture of the position of women in the post-independence period. She said : 'Most marriages are still forced unions. Fathers are still all-powerful and can interrupt at will the studies of their daughters. If one must be able to earn one's living in order to be free, how can Algerian women be free? There are less than 1,000 salaried women employed in agriculture and even fewer in industry; they are just as scarce in administration. In the P T T (Post Office Department) which employs by far the greatest number, female personnel account for about one eighth of a total of about 1,400; 1,100 women work in the Ministry of Education, 68 in the Foreign Office, 26 in the Ministry of Youth, and 20 in the Ministry of Tourism. And most of them are cleaning women or typists.'[10]

Yet observers note that whenever political rallies are held women attend in large numbers, showing that they are politically aware. On 8 March 1965, International Women's Day, U N F A organized a mass rally and demonstration, and the people of Algiers were startled to see 10,000 women of all ages marching as one in the streets. The men who watched could not believe their eyes. However, this magnificent rally was not followed up with similar rallies in other cities.

It was easy to recognize the oppressor in the French administrator and colon. It was not so easy to do so with the head of a family in a patriarchal system. The revolution had set in motion a process to wipe out prejudices which had become encrusted over centuries. But after the revolution, conservatism again surrounded the gains the women made during the revolution. Even if the contradictions are not antagonistic, in general, the male is not prepared to give up his privileged position in the household without a fight.

However, the oppressed position of the women in Algeria as well as in other parts of Africa, has its economic side as well. Independence left Algeria with a weak economic base. Every year, thousands of Algerians continue to cross over to France in search of employment. There is still a scramble for jobs. Under such conditions, the woman has to fight her way into the economic system.

In recent times, the Algerian government has banked on the younger generation of girls, educated in modern and often co-educational schools, to spearhead the struggle for the total emancipation of women. What favours them is the government's plan for Algeria to break from the ranks of developing nations and move into the orbit of the developed. It is believed that Algeria can achieve the so-called economic miracle. If so, then Algeria will once again need the full and active participation of women.

11
TO 'PUT AFRICA IN MOTION'

To put Africa in motion, to co-operate in its organization, in its regrouping behind revolutionary principles, to participate in the ordered movement of a continent – this was really the work I had chosen.[1]

As the Algerian war dragged on, it became increasingly difficult to keep the A L N supplied with adequate arms and munitions. The problem was intensified when the French General Challe ordered the laying of minefields along Algeria's frontiers with Tunisia and Morocco. Fanon suffered personally as a result of this manoeuvre. In 1959, he was travelling in a jeep which hit a mine on the Algerian-Morocco border. He suffered severe back injuries and had to go to Rome for medical treatment. While in hospital there, assassins broke into the room they thought he was occupying, and fired at the empty bed. If he had not moved to another room the day before, he would almost certainly have been killed.

In March 1960, Fanon became the representative of the Provisional Government of Algeria in Accra. It was his main task to establish a base south of the Sahara and to organize the sending of supplies to the A L N by way of Mali. The recognition of the G P R A by Nkrumah, and his strong support for freedom fighters, had made Accra an obvious headquarters for the West African operation.

Having attended conferences in Bamako and Cotonou between 1957 and 1958, and more important, the All-African Peoples' Conference in Accra in December 1958, Fanon was no stranger to West Africa. He had met Nkrumah and was greatly inspired and influenced by his revolutionary Pan-Africanism. In Ghana, Fanon met freedom fighters from all parts of the African continent who had been given sanctuary by the Nkrumah government, and who were training and organizing for the liberation of their countries. Among them was Félix Moumié, President of U P C (Union of the Populations of the Cameroons). Moumié made a profound impression on Fanon and they became close friends. The news of Moumié's death from poisoning by imperialist agents while on a visit to Geneva, reached Fanon while he was in Accra.

Fanon later wrote in his notebook of the reaction of Moumié's father to his son's death and to Fanon's words of comfort: 'Progressively the father yielded place to the militant. Yes, he said, the programme is clear. We must stick to the programme.'[2] After the initial shock and anguish, there was to be no despondency, no slackening of the struggle.

The deep sorrow of losing comrades, often under the most tragic circumstances, is all a part of revolutionary experience. But Fanon, with his great sensitivity, must have suffered exceptional mental torture at such times. Soon after Moumié's death he had to face up to the murder of another dear friend. This time it was Patrice Lumumba, born the same year as Fanon, and whose struggle in the Congo, Fanon saw as part of the same struggle being waged by the F L N in Algeria.

But Fanon had immense resources of courage, determination and confidence to draw upon. He envisaged an Africa which would one day be completely liberated and unified. He called it: 'This Africa to come.'[3] At the same time, he was evolving the conception of a wider unity between all the oppressed peoples of Africa, Asia and Latin America, the so-called Third World. Expressing his determination to carry on the fight he declared that the war must be taken to the enemy who must be given no respite until victory had been achieved.

Fanon had been chosen by the G P R A to be its representative in Accra in recognition of his identification with the African revolution as a whole, and his special knowledge of black Africa. While some members of the F L N leadership looked rather to the Maghreb states than to black Africa, Fanon invariably thought first of co-operation with African states. He was passionately concerned with the effect of the Algerian liberation struggle on the African Revolution. If the Algerian national liberation struggle succeeded then it would be a severe setback to imperialist and neocolonialist interests in other parts of the continent.

Fanon wrote many well-informed articles in *El Moudjahid* on political and economic problems in sub-Sahara Africa. Clearly, he was very much aware of the reactionary role of the bourgeoisie particularly in the state machinery and in the economic life of the African states. He warned his readers of the dangers of neocolonialism and of the continued balkanization of Africa. While his travels and experience served to strengthen his complete faith in the ordinary people of Africa, he became increasingly critical of leaders such as Houphouet-Boigny of Ivory Coast and Leopold Senghor of Senegal. He described the former as a lackey of the French government, and Senghor as a slave of European culture. Fanon regarded Ghana, Guinea and Mali under the revolutionary leadership of Kwame Nkrumah, Sékou Touré and Modibo Keita respectively as the most progressive states in Africa. The Congo (now Zaire) under Patrice Lumumba's brief leadership was included in the same category. In this connection, it is of interest to note that Fanon's view of the key position of Zaire in Africa is identical with the views expressed on many occasions by Nkrumah. In the words of Fanon: 'Let us be sure never to forget it; the fate of all of us is at stake in the Congo.'[4] Nkrumah in his book *Challenge of the Congo*, and in many speeches and broadcasts declared that, 'the troubles of the Congo are . . . our troubles, and her struggles are those of the independent states of Africa'.[5] He pointed out that geographically Zaire occupies a strategic position as regards the whole of central and southern Africa. Its vast resources if in the hands of the people of Zaire could be a decisive factor in the anti-imperialist struggle in southern Africa. But if allowed to be exploited by the enemies of the African people these same resources could be a formidable obstacle in the path of the advancing African Revolution.

Lumumba visited Tunis in 1960 and met leading members of the G P R A. *El Moudjahid* marked the occasion with a special editorial, and in the 5 August issue quoted Lumumba on the subject of the Algerian revolution:

The Algerian problem for us, is the problem of all of Africa that is struggling for its liberation. Africa is not opposed to the West, Africa has no hatred for the white man. Africa has its right to dignity and liberty in the same fashion as all the countries of the world.

For us there is no French Algeria. There is Algeria, that is all, and this Algeria is in the African continent.

Like Fanon and the F L N, Lumumba held the view that African states and the states of the Maghreb should not get involved in the Cold War. They should concentrate all their efforts on the total liberation of their peoples from political and economic oppression.

At the All-African Peoples' Conference in Accra in 1960, Fanon made a notable speech as representative of the G P R A. A witness of that speech, Peter Worsley, said that Fanon spoke with great brilliance and passion, and at one point seemed almost to break down. Questioned afterwards, Fanon explained that he had suddenly felt 'overcome at the thought that he had to stand there, before the assembled representatives of African nationalist movements, to try and persuade them that the Algerian cause was important, at a time when men were dying and being tortured in his country for a cause whose justice ought to command automatic support from rational and progressive human beings'.[8]

During 1960, Fanon and seven companions, each a specialist in his particular sphere of operations, travelled thousands of miles throughout West Africa, sometimes by air but more often by road, making contacts, studying local conditions and organizing supplies. On several occasions they narrowly escaped capture by French intelligence agents. As they journeyed from Accra to Bamako, Conakry, Cotonou, Timbuktu, Mopti, Gao, Bouressa, Tamanrasset, and to many other places some of which could only be reached after exhausting drives along dirt roads or mere tracks through the bush, they faced perpetual danger. On one occasion, they had to disguise themselves as Arabs to cross territory in the Sahara held by the French, in order to make contact with a Malian nomad group. Another time, their mission would have been brought to an abrupt end if at the last minute they had not decided to cancel their flight on a French aircraft bound from Monrovia for Conakry. The aircraft was diverted to Abidjan, and was there searched by French forces, with the connivance of the Ivory Coast President, Houphouet-Boigny, who 'continues to play a leading role in the French colonial system'.[6] On yet another occasion, this time in northern Mali, their car was stopped by officious policemen, who demanded their passports, and questioned them about their journey. It was only after Fanon had grown very angry, and had challenged them to arrest him for refusal to present his papers that they eventually let them go and promised absolute silence.

Their mission, to open the southern front, to stir up the people living in the southern Sahara, and to arrange for the transport of arms from Mali, was very urgent. They received enthusiastic support in Guinea from President Sékou Touré, and in Mali from President Modibo Keita. But it was not an easy matter to ensure the safety of the actual supply routes. Yet this had to be accomplished if the A L N was to be adequately supplied. Fanon wrote in his notebook: 'We must work fast. Time presses. The enemy is still stubborn. In reality he does not believe in military defeat. But I have never felt it so possible, so within reach.'[7]

Day after day, night after night, the tensions and strains of travelling under extremely difficult conditions, with very little rest, and always faced with the danger of discovery or betrayal, began to take their toll. Fanon, never sparing himself, and filled with a driving sense of urgency and responsibility for the comrades fighting in Algeria, taxed his physical resources to the utmost. He returned from the mission exhausted, having lost a lot of weight. He had, it seems, contracted leukaemia.

12
FANON AND THE REFORMIST POLITICAL PARTY

The party should be the direct expression of the masses. The party is not an administration responsible for transmitting government orders; it is the energetic spokesman and the incorruptible defender of the masses.[1]

WHILE Fanon was travelling throughout West Africa, organising supply routes south of the Sahara for the A L N, he was constantly turning over in his mind some of the major problems facing the oppressed in their fight for freedom. He was particularly concerned with problems of organization, the composition of national liberation movements, their objectives, and the question of armed struggle. When he knew that he was suffering from leukaemia, and had only a short time to live, he further taxed his failing strength by writing down his analyses and conclusions on these important problems in the hope that they might be of assistance to those engaged in the revolutionary struggle. These writings were published under the title *The Wretched of the Earth*, shortly before he died.

In this book, Fanon devotes a great deal of attention to the nationalist political party, both before and after, independence. 'The national political parties never lay stress upon the necessity of a trial of strength, for the good reason that their objective is not the radical overthrowing of the system.'[2]

He analyses the Gandhian political party as it operated in Africa, and examines its policies, tactics and ideas both before and after independence. In both stages he has nothing good to say about it. Looking at it from the standpoint of a revolutionary nationalist, he shows up its leadership to be ideologically shallow, timid, and opportunistic in the extreme. He lashed out at it at a time when this type of political party in Africa was being widely praised as the authentic voice of the national movement. Though the leaders did little to mobilize the entire people, they were not slow in taking upon themselves the responsibility of speaking for the entire people. Fanon's observations were without any specific or detailed reference to any single party. Nevertheless the merit of his analysis, which is essentially critical, lies in that events have proved him to be correct and its apologists wrong.

Linking the policy of the party of non-violence with the bourgeoisie, Fanon writes: 'At the decisive moment, the colonialist bourgeoisie, which up till then has remained inactive, comes into the field. It introduces that new idea ... non-violence. In its simplest form this non-violence signifies to the intellectual and economic *élite* of the colonized country that the bourgeoisie has the same interests as them ... Non-violence is an attempt to settle the colonial problem around a green baize table.'[3] The aim of such a political party is not to overthrow the system. The leaders, however, in order to deceive the masses, shout a few high sounding slogans vague enough to be acceptable to both the rulers and the people. A characteristic feature of such political parties is that they proclaim certain abstract principles but do not issue definite commands. Under colonialism, these nationalist political parties confine themselves to constitutional methods. The members talk in general terms of the rights of people to self-determination and the rights of man to freedom from hunger and to human dignity. The tactics of such a party cannot be separated from its basic aim which is to achieve political power while maintaining capitalism. The struggle had very well and carefully defined limits. If action is taken, it is in the form of stoppages of work in the few industries which have been set up in the towns, in mass demonstrations, and in the boycotting of imported goods.

Fanon compares the attitude of the leaders of such a nationalist reformist party to the crucial question of armed struggle. 'On the specific question of violence the *élite* are ambiguous. They are violent in their words and reformist in their attitudes. When the nationalist political leaders *say* something, they make quite clear that they do not really *think* it.'[4]

Fanon exposes the opportunism of leaders who capitalize on the sacrifices of the people in order to wring concessions for themselves from the rulers. 'The majority of nationalist parties have not written into their propaganda the necessity for armed intervention. They do not oppose the continuing of the rebellion, but they content themselves with leaving it to the spontaneous action of the country people. As a whole they treat this new element as a sort of manna fallen from heaven, and pray to goodness that it'll go on falling.'[5] However, they do not identify themselves with the people's resistance. They very seldom join the freedom fighters. To the colonial power they say that they are still capable of stopping the slaughter, and that the masses still have confidence in them. Yet they proclaim that they have nothing to do with 'terrorists'.

The essential political position of such a leadership is that it seeks to effect a compromise between the oppressor and the people in the spirit of give-and-take. But it is not compromise between equals at the negotiating table, or compromise which would advance the interests of the people. It is a compromise which saves for imperialism its system of exploitation while it gains for the political leadership its class political power. This compromise thus barters the rights of the people for privileges and concessions for a small minority. In the words of Fanon: 'Compromise involves the colonial system and the young nationalist bourgeoisie . . . (who) are genuinely afraid of being swept away by this huge hurricane.'[6] It is for this reason too, that they keep on saying: ' "This is very serious! We do not know how it will end; we must find a solution – some sort of compromise." '[7] The result of the sacrifices of the people, and the secret conferences and tea parties of the leaders, is that the reformist leaders are made to seem genuine freedom fighters. Fanon could well have been writing about Algeria, for that is just what was taking place in the F L N while he was writing the book. The bourgeoisie, under the leadership of Ferhat Abbas, then taking over control of the F L N, was beginning to open negotiations with De Gaulle.

Fanon noted that even before independence there exists within the reformist party a revolutionary minority which challenges the leadership: 'They begin to question their leaders ceaselessly on crucial points: "What is nationalism? What sense do you give to this word? What is its meaning?

Independence for what?" [8] They are ready to suggest that constitutional methods should be supplemented by 'all other means'. 'After the first skirmishes, the official leaders speedily dispose of this effervescence which they are quick to label as childishness . . . The official leaders, draped in their years of experience, will pitilessly disown these "adventurers and anarchists".'[9] Fanon describes the composition of this minority as those who have worked their way up from the bottom, are often unskilled workers, seasonal labourers and even sometimes chronically unemployed. For them, the fact of militating in a national party is not simply taking part in politics; it is choosing the only means whereby they can pass from the status of an animal to that of a human being. It is this revolutionary section of the party leadership which is marked out for the severest repression by the rulers. They are not spared, for from them emanate ideas that the people must fight not only for political independence, but also, to change the system. Imprisoned, often tortured, these leaders use their time in prison to clarify their ideas, and to strengthen their determination.

On the other hand, the reformist leaders, knowing that the rulers are on their side, or sometimes at the instigation of the rulers, come down on the revolutionary minority: 'We can observe the process whereby the rupture occurs between the illegal and legal tendencies in the party. The illegal minority (which believes in armed struggle) is made to feel that they are undesirables . . . The repression of these wayward elements intensifies as the legal party draws nearer to colonialism.'[10] Here then is the beginning of the eventual parting of the ways after independence. In many cases, the revolutionary minority is precluded from forming a workers' and peasants' party by legislation which allows only one party to exist. The revolutionary minority is driven underground, moving the centre of its activities from the towns to the countryside.

The national political party is an instrument used by the bourgeoisie to wrest political power from the colonialists. But after independence, its principal purpose having been achieved, the party begins to wither and decay. Fanon records this phenomenon and describes the disintegration. 'Nothing is left but the shell of a party, the name, the emblem and the motto.'[11] Despite the limitations stated by Fanon, the party is recognized by the people as their organization. But with independence in the hands of the reformist party the state machinery becomes an instrument of oppression and exploitation. While other fields are neglected, the rulers perfect this instrument.

There are, therefore, two organizations on the eve of independence, the party and the state machinery. Formerly, they were in opposition to each other. With independence, their functions become complementary, and the paramount question then is, which controls which? Does the party control the government? Or does the state machinery control the party? Fanon states that after independence it is the party which suffers, for it 'sinks into an extraordinary lethargy. The militants are only called upon when so-called popular manifestations are afoot, or international conferences, or independence celebrations. The local party leaders are given administrative posts, the party becomes an administration'.[12] The party becomes a means of private advancement. Like the state machinery which is used by the bourgeoisie for its own selfish interests. The party turns against the people. In a severe indictment Fanon exposes its new role: 'The party helps the government to hold the people down. It becomes more and more clearly anti-democratic, an implement of coercion.'[13] He returns to the same point again later in the book when he says that the party is given the task of controlling the masses: 'The party acts as a barometer and as an information service. The militant is turned into an informer'.[14]

Over a decade has passed since Fanon made these observations and events have proved his main observations so correct that they could well have been made today. The independence parties which still exist have in most cases become shadows of their former selves. In general, they are wilting and decaying and are only brought to life when elections are imminent. The political party which led the national movement for independence is no longer a force in African politics. In many countries they have been banned after military juntas have overthrown the civilian governments. Only in a very few cases do the parties of pre-independence show vitality, but even they are weakened because the state machinery has claimed their most experienced leaders, and is continually luring the youth into government service. It is rare to see a pre-independence party leader devoting much attention to party work. He is both a government leader and a party leader. As a result, it is not government work which suffers but party work.

A few years after independence, many civilian governments headed by the national parties were overthrown. Except in a few instances, like Ghana, where there was not only resistance to the overthrow, but struggle continued after the coup, there was hardly any active response from the people. In most cases, the people did not rise up to defend their party or their leaders. The reason was that they had ceased to regard the party and its leaders as their own. Independence did not bring about any real alleviation of their positions, while many of the leaders amassed wealth and power. The people thus were not prepared to shed their blood any more to defend a corrupt and self-seeking leadership. In the main, therefore, they greeted the coups with either indifference or with relief.

The bourgeoisie, which Fanon so dramatically exposes in *The Wretched of the Earth*, downgrades the role of the political party. Only the triumph of socialist ideas will allow the formation of a vanguard party as a true expression of the people.

13
PROBLEMS OF LEADERSHIP

What is of decisive importance is that the Party's political line must be the revolutionary line of the working class, one which embodies the latter's stand and viewpoint. If the Party deviates from this political stand and viewpoint the revolution is bound to fail.[1]

THOSE who advocate the leadership of the working class in the national democratic movement do so because in the era of imperialism and neocolonialism, it is only this class which can lead the struggle against feudalism and imperialism to the end. It alone can eliminate tribalism, medievalism, feudalism and imperialism and neocolonialism, because it is in its own interests to do so.

Fanon agreed with the thesis that the national bourgeoisie is incapable of constructing a new society and of eliminating feudalism and tribalism. He believed that it was totally incapable of leading society forward. Not only was it ideologically bankrupt, but it was failing to develop production sufficiently. It was not in a position to weld the various tribes into a nation. It had forfeited, therefore, its right to leadership in the national democratic revolution. There is no more withering exposure of the national bourgeoisie than that in Fanon's book *The Wretched of the Earth*.

But Fanon was faced with the question of, who was to lead the national movement, if not the bourgeoisie? Just as Fanon categorically rejected the bourgeoisie, he equally rejected the working class as fit for leadership of the movement: 'It cannot be too strongly stressed that in the colonial territories the proletariat is the nucleus of the colonized population which has been most pampered by the colonial regime. The embryonic proletariat of the towns is in a comparatively privileged position. In capitalist countries, the working class has nothing to lose; it is they who in the long run have everything to gain. In the colonial countries the working class has everything to lose.'[2] He arrives at the conclusion that the peasants are the only revolutionary part of the population, and therefore, by implication, it is they who must lead the revolution in the national democratic phase: 'It is clear that in the colonial countries the peasants alone are revolutionary, for they have nothing to lose and everything to gain. The starving peasant, outside the class system, is the first among the exploited to discover that only violence pays.'[3]

The penetration of capitalism into feudal and tribal societies, upsetting the balance which existed from time immemorial, and later the conquest of these territories in the era of imperialism, certainly turned the peasantry along the road to revolution. And at the base of most national liberation movements is the agrarian question and the demand of the peasants for land. But Fanon's thesis, that the peasantry is the only truly revolutionary class and that the lumpenproletariat is its main ally, has laid him open to criticism from those who maintain that socialist revolution can only be achieved through the leadership of the proletariat and revolutionary intellectuals, who of course rally the support of the peasantry, but who are themselves the main revolutionary force.

While Fanon's sweeping generalizations and unorthodox conclusions make him an easy target for Marxist critics, it is nevertheless necessary to study Fanon not only in the light of the experience of the African peoples, but also in the context of the peoples' struggles in other parts of the world, notably in Asia. For Fanon, in *The Wretched of the Earth,* had in mind the oppressed of the whole of the 'Third World'.

The obvious example of a people's war in which the peasantry played a major role was in Vietnam. In 1966, Le Duan, Secretary of the Vietnamese Workers' Party, endorsing Fanon's view of the agrarian basis of the national liberation movement said: 'In a colony with an overwhelmingly peasant population the problem of democratic rights is, in essence, the land problem. Failing to solve it, we could not mobilize the labouring peasantry in the struggle against imperialism, for national independence. "National independence", and "land to the tillers" are two closely related mottos and the fundamental contents of the national democratic revolution.'[4] The peasants in Vietnam, as in most colonies, constitute more than 90 per cent of the population. They have been the backbone of every major rebellion and struggle against colonialism in Vietnam. Recording this, Le Duan says: 'The 1930 uprising to set up Soviet power in Nge An was essentially an insurrection of peasants; the biggest force participating in the 1936-39 democratic movement was also the peasant; the Nank Ky, Bac Son uprisings were fundamentally waged by the peasants . . . the August 1945 general insurrection to seize power was an uprising of the entire population and the majority of them were the peasants. Our protracted resistance war which lasted nine years was basically a guerrilla war waged by the peasants.'[5]

The same could well be said of the war aimed at expelling the American aggressor from Vietnam, and of unifying the country. It was a peasants' war. Martin Bernal, after his visit to Vietnam in 1972 wrote: 'The Vietnamese Revolution has been the most effective mobilization of the peasants and of tribal peoples in world history.'[6]

If there is one consistent thread which runs throughout Fanon's writings from *Black Skin and White Masks* to his final work, *The Wretched of the Earth,* it is his enthusiasm for the struggle of the Vietnamese people. In fact, he wanted Vietnam to be a model for all the colonies fighting for liberation. Yet Fanon never really understood the inner dynamics of the Vietnamese revolution. He never defined accurately those who were physically involved in the struggle, and the political line of the leadership directing it. The fact is that the Vietnamese Workers' Party, and the N L F (National Liberation Front) in South Vietnam which have been able to mobilize the peasantry to a level unknown in history, were guided by a political line which upheld the dominant role of the working class in the national front, the organizational expression of the national democratic movement. This puzzled Bernal and those like him, for it appeared paradoxical that 'those who have created the most successful and tenacious peasant revolutionary movement in world history should be firmly wedded to the leadership of the working class which made up less than 3 per cent of the population in 1945'.[7]

Since the national movement in Vietnam was to embrace

the entire nation, willing to fight French imperalism, since it could not exclude any class but had to embrace all, the key question then was which class should lead it? Ho Chi Minh said: 'The working class is the most courageous and revolutionary class which unflinchingly and fearlessly stands up to the imperialists and colonialists. Armed with a vanguard revolutionary doctrine, and the experience of the international proletarian movement our working class has proved itself to be the most deserving and trustworthy leader of the Vietnamese people.'[8]

Truong-Chinh in his address on the 150th birthday of Karl Marx posed the same question, and answered as follows: 'Who in Vietnamese society was to overthrow the imperialists and feudalists? It was the four classes among the people: the working class, the peasantry, the petty bourgeoisie and the national bourgeoisie, but essentially it was the working class and the peasantry . . . Leadership over the Vietnamese revolution must belong to the working class, for it is the most advanced and the most thoroughly revolutionary class; the working class alone is qualified for leading the Vietnamese revolution to total victory.'[9]

The Indo-Chinese Communist Party fought the erroneous tendency peddled by certain sections of the petty bourgeoisie, that the leadership of the revolution should be in the hands of a common front of all classes. The point here is not to deny the revolutionary nature of the peasantry, but rather to see that the leadership of the national democratic movement is not seized by the bourgeoisie. The Vietnamese maintained that the proletariat and not the bourgeoisie, should lead the revolutionary peasantry to victory. Without peasant participation and involvement there could be no real revolution. Thus the party upheld the 'worker-peasant alliance' within the national front: 'There can be no National United Front without the worker-peasant alliance . . . National liberation can only be truly revolutionary when its core is made up of the workers and peasants, when it develops with the power of the worker-peasant alliance and under the leadership of the working-class.'[10] The worker-peasant alliance then was regarded as a pre-condition for victory in the national democratic revolution.

The Vietnamese, unlike Fanon, did not idolize the peasant. They understood him. They recognized his revolutionary potentiality, but also knew his position in an economy which was built on small-scale production. It is this type of production which has no place under capitalism in its monopoly stage, for like the small businessman and industrialist, the small-scale farmer is being eliminated under monopoly capitalism. The future solution of the peasant's problem of land hunger and starvation lies not in individual private ownership, but in collective farming using modern, scientific methods. The methods of production used by the proletariat, the use of machinery, of the concentration of social labour within a unit, has to be used by the peasantry. In other words, the working class can lead the peasantry to a new form of relationship in production, of social and collective labour, which will free him from impoverishment and insecurity.

The Vietnamese Workers' Party knew that its own history contained many peasant revolts against this or that feudal ruler. But these rebellions did not lead to revolutions. They did not change the economic structure of society. If the rebellion was successful it led to a change in dynasty, with feudal relationships remaining intact. In fact, these rebellions stabilized the feudal structure, by infusing healthy nomadic and peasant blood into the decrepid and anaemic feudal dynasties. The only occasions when the peasants succeeded in making a revolution which altered economic relations in society, were when they were led by another class. For example, the French Revolution in 1789 was historic precisely because the change of government, the overthrow of a monarchy, also led to a basic change in society. Feudalism was overthrown by capitalism. Here, the peasants were led by the bourgeoisie. In 1917 in Russia, peasants participated in the revolution when the bourgeoisie was overthrown. But the peasants were led by the working class. Far from the peasantry alone leading the revolution, history has shown again and again that the peasants single-handed cannot change the economic structure of society. The real practical question of our epoch is whether it is the proletariat or the national bourgeoisie that is to lead the national democratic revolution. The Vietnamese experience has confirmed that the national democratic revolution can only be thorough, with feudalism being torn out root and branch, if it is led by the working class. The bourgeoisie has shown itself incapable of carrying out a thorough-going agrarian programme. Freedom under its leadership means national independence without land to the peasants.

The Algerian experience also repudiates Fanon's thesis that the peasants are the only revolutionary class. If this was valid, then as a class they would lead the national liberation front, and on independence, would realize their demands, namely 'land to the tiller'. But even at the Soumman Conference where their pressure was the strongest, they were not able to get a clear resolution passed about their demand for land, although Conference members paid tribute to their sacrifices in the revolution. On independence, only the land of the colon, which represented only about one third of the total land of Algeria was given to the peasant. That, too, only after a struggle, for if the Ben Khedda wing or the Ferhat Abbas wing had been triumphant, then even the land of the colons would not have been given to them. Landlordism and feudalism remained untouched for almost ten years after independence. In this period, over 650,000 Algerians left the country for France as migrant workers, as in colonial times. These workers were, in reality, landless peasants.

However, the question that is causing discussion and debate amongst revolutionaries is, in what way does the working class lead the revolution in the colonies and newly independent countries? Fanon's description of the working class in the colonies, which he branded as privileged, consisted of transport workers, taxi drivers, miners, dockers, nurses, entrepreneurs and others. He reckoned that these were the bourgeois section of the colonized population.

However, the modern proletariat which is the revolutionary class, is in a key position because of its position in the processes of production in a capitalist society. The working class occupies the decisive sectors of the economy. Therefore, like the bourgeoisie, the working class is also a product of historical development. Ever since the introduction of private property, there have always been people who have been landless, and who have had nothing but their labour power to sell. The modern proletariat however, is part of a system of production where labour has reached such a stage that no one worker can say, 'this is *my* product'. The product that emerges from the factory is a social product, the result of the collective effort of all the workers in a factory. Such a system of production uses machinery on a large scale. Such a system keeps on expanding, using increasingly advanced science and technology. Hitherto, mankind remained backward because productivity was low, and therefore it was not possible to support a large section of the population which was not engaged in direct production. But with modern means of production, the proletariat can support millions in society who are not involved in direct production.

The revolutionary position of the proletariat under capitalism and in the colonies developed from the fact that while they produced by their collective labour immense wealth for society, the wealth was appropriated by a relatively few individuals. The great contradiction of capitalist society has been that while production is social, appropriation is individual. This has led to the working class adopting a revolutionary position, for objectively the operation of this contradiction necessitates change. The key sectors the proletariat occupies in the economy are the factories, mines, construction industries and transport. In a colonial society, in addition to these sectors there are the large plantations, employing the rural proletariat.

The significance of Marx and Engels is that they provided the modern proletariat with an ideology which could be applied to specific conditions. It armed it with ideas to make it conscious of its key role in modern society and to reveal its strength. They worked out a system of thought from which flowed a political line which would advance the cause of the working class.

Lenin's contribution lay in fashioning the organization which the working class could use in order to conquer political power. It was not a question of admitting into the organization every worker, but only those who were conscious of class interests, and who were prepared to discipline themselves to promote class interests. He evolved the idea of a tightly disciplined party which was to be the vanguard movement of the workers. The party had no other interest but to serve the working class on whom it relied for its strength and power. A vanguard party was necessary, because the bourgeoisie had brought into the political scene political parties which were supposed to represent the interests of the workers. Some of them attracted a large number of workers, but these parties followed the politics of the bourgeoisie. In Lenin's time, the issue was not how many workers there were in an organization, but whether the political line followed the interests of the proletariat. As it happened, the party of the working class, the Bolshevik Party, did have the support of the mass of the working class, but the decisive factor was the political line.

This became evident when the First World War broke out. The socialist parties in the Second International, which boasted the membership of millions of workers were faced with what to do when the war broke out. Would they join with their bourgeoisie and be a party to the slaughter of thousands of workers? Or would they join their fellow workers of other countries and turn the imperialist war into a class war? Lenin and others took a political line in the interests of the working class and condemned the war and called upon workers to turn against the bourgeoisie. This meant following a political line which would advance the workers' interests even if it meant flowing against the stream, for some workers were misled by false notions of patriotism. The socialist parties, however, despite resolutions that they would not support an imperialist war, joined their respective bourgeoisies and became parties to the slaughter of their fellow workers. This was a blow to the cause of proletarian solidarity.

During the time of Marx and Engels there were a number of tendencies within the working-class movement which competed for the allegiance of the workers. After the 1917 Russian Revolution, the question of which ideology was dominant in the working-class movement was settled once and for all. There could be only the possibility of a revision of Marxism-Leninism. Lenin did not apply Marxism mechanically and wait for capitalism to mature, but struck at imperialism's weakest link. In this, he creatively applied Marxism. It was an urban revolution, with the working class leading the peasantry.

Ho Chi Minh and Mao Tse Tung creatively applied Marxism to the realities of their respective countries. They considered that the weak link of imperialism lay primarily in the countryside, and not in the towns. It could be the countryside which could be transformed into a base for revolution. The leadership of the working class lay in its channelling of the resistance and rebellion of the peasantry and turning it into a revolution. The political line of the working class underwent modification, and the struggle was to be two-phased. The first phase was to be national democratic. The second was to be socialist. As the leadership was in the hands of the working class, the transition period of the elimination of imperialism and feudalism to a period of socialism leading eventually to communism, would not be very long.

In Vietnam, the workers showed great revolutionary heroism in their struggle against oppressors and exploiters. But unlike the Russian workers, they were not in a position to capture power in the cities. Imperialists and capitalists too had learnt their lesson from 1917. Under such reality, the correct political line to advance the interests of the working class was to find the weakest link in the armour of imperialism, and this undoubtedly lay in the countryside. The working class had to merge with the peasants, like yeast mingling with dough. The working class thus became a catalyst in the national struggle, bringing with them the culture, class consciousness, scientific knowledge, discipline, and technical know-how: learned in a capitalist society. Most important of all, the working class brought to the national democratic movement, the proletarian ideology of Marxism-Leninism, and applied it to Vietnam. It brought also its organization, the well-disciplined politically-aware party.

A party in a colonial country, engaging in guerrilla warfare in the countryside, would of necessity have the workers in a minority. This was the case in Vietnam. Yet it would be able to fulfil its task because its political line is that of the working class, and also because its cadres, drawn from the ranks of the poor peasants, the rural proletariat and small farmers, have become so politically-conscious and disciplined, that they have become 'proletarianized', and are therefore prepared to carry out, and to defend the political line of the working class. This is in direct contrast to parties which have millions of workers as members, but whose political line is that of the bourgeoisie. The leaders of such parties have infected the workers with the ideas of the bourgeoisie.

Fanon took the controversial view that the countryside, this vast arena in the three continents of Asia, Africa and Latin America constitutes imperialism's weakest link. The correct political line in such a situation is for the working-class party to forge a worker-peasant alliance, and to shift the centre of action from the towns to the countryside. This is not revising scientific socialism but applying it to the living realities of the situation.

Eduardo Mondlane, founder of Frelino, recognized this supreme reality. The workers had come out in a series of strikes in Mozambique which shook the rulers. The first one was in 1947, and the other in 1962-63. Despite heroism and sacrifice these strikes were brutally and savagely suppressed. Mondlane remarked: 'Its failure and the brutal repression which followed in every instance have temporarily discouraged both the masses and the leadership from considering strike action as a possible effective political weapon in the context of Mozambique.' " Showing where the revolution should face he said: 'The urban population of Mozambique amounts altogether to less than half a million. A nationalist movement without firm roots in the countryside could never hope to succeed.'[12]

The abstention of certain working-class parties from the national democratic phase, or their concentration principally in the urban areas, has resulted in bourgeois elements seizing the leadership of the national struggle in its armed phase. Had the Algerian Communist Party given support to the struggle, or had it launched the struggle, there is little doubt that independence would have gone hand in hand with 'land to the tiller'. For the proletariat is the only reliable ally of the peasant. Revolutions cannot wait for objective conditions to mature, that is, for the growth of a large and concentrated working class. It did not wait in the case of Russia. It did not wait in China, Vietnam, Korea, Cuba, Albania, or in East European countries. It is not waiting in Africa.

14
THE BATTLE OF THE MIND

Colonialism and its derivatives do not, as a matter of fact, constitute the present enemies of Africa. In a short time this continent will be liberated. For my part, the deeper I enter into the cultures and the political circles, the surer I am that the great danger that threatens Africa is the absence of ideology.[1]

THE national liberation movement is in a favourable position to win the battle of the mind, for being part of the people it expresses their aspirations for a need to change society. But in the intervening period not only has it to convince them that change is desirable, but that change is in fact taking place, and that victory for the cause must come sooner or later. The people need to be convinced that their sacrifices and sufferings are not in vain, and that genuine, fundamental social change will result.

In the tribal era of resistance and struggle, the people were not able to comprehend the workings of the capitalist system. Capitalism had unleashed productive forces undreamt of by the colonial people. In their fight the people had not only to contend with the gun, the visible superiority, but also the organization that went with it. For instance, even before the first shot was fired, the internal unity of the tribe was already undermined because teachers, traders and missionaries had already won over a section of the people.

The participation of intellectuals in national liberation movements meant that the people had at their disposal those who were able to analyse the workings of the capitalist system, to know its strength as well as its weakness, to know who were the peoples' allies and who were their enemies. Most important of all, the people were able to use those ideas and institutions, weapons and organizations found in the capitalist system as tools for their own emancipation.

In Algeria, two such tools were the radio and the French language. Fanon wrote about the use the revolutionaries made of the radio as an instrument to cement national unity. Before 1945, 95 per cent of receivers were in the hands of Europeans. The Algerians who owned radios belonged to the bourgeoisie and included a number of Kabyles who had formerly emigrated to France and who had returned to their villages. There were hundreds of Algerian families who had the means to own a radio, but who nevertheless did not possess one. The radio to them was regarded as essentially an instrument of the colonial masters designed to propagate the values, culture and mores of the dominant group in society. 'Radio Alger,' the French broadcasting station established in Algeria for decades, was regarded as spokesman of the colonial world. Before the war the Algerian described Radio Alger as 'Frenchmen speaking to Frenchmen'.[2]

The Algerian nationalists, after the launching of armed struggle, were faced with the problem of how to keep the population informed of the progress as well as the pace of the revolution. In the early stages they used the democratic press in Algiers. But this was soon silenced or subject to heavy censorship. Therefore, the revolution had to evolve ways and means to counter the lies of the rulers. The people were given doses of information from only one side. They knew that much of it was lies, and they were eager to know the version of the F L N on a particular event, or its stand on a particular issue. The Algerian nationalist came into contact with a people eager to know the truth. It was necessary, therefore, to oppose enemy 'news' with authentic news disseminated by the F L N.

Even before the people used the press and radio, they had evolved their own media of communication. In many parts of Africa this kind of news dissemination has been called the 'bush telegraph'. In Algeria, the French spoke of the 'Arab telephone'. This was a tribute to the speed with which messages were passed among the people. Algerians began to buy radios to know the truth. They tuned in to Cairo, Tunis, and to other Arab capitals to find out what was taking place in Algeria. But it was at the end of 1956, that a real advance was made. Leaflets were distributed announcing the existence of a new radio transmitting station, the 'Voice of Free Algeria'. Broadcasting schedules and wavelengths were given. In less than three weeks the entire stock of radio sets in Algeria was bought up.

The purchase of a radio by the Algerian, after 1956, was a political act, for it symbolized not only the adoption of a modern apparatus for getting news, but gave access to the only means of entering into communication with the revolution. In the words of Fanon: 'The Voice of Fighting Algeria was to be of capital importance in consolidating and unifying the people.'[3]

With the establishment of the 'Voice of Free Algeria', the war was now spread from the battlefields in the mountains, cities and plains, to the realm of the mind. Ideas fought ideas with the same intensity and ferocity as in actual military combat. Fanon described the impact the 'Voice' made on the people. 'From one village to the next, from one shack to the next, the "Voice of Algeria" would recount new things, tell of more and more glorious battles, picture vividly the collapse of the occupying power . . . Thus the Voice of Algeria . . . which was tracked by the adversary's powerful jamming networks, and whose "word" was often inaudible, nourished the citizen's faith in the Revolution.'[4]

Clear proof that the French were put on the defensive with the establishment of the 'Voice' were the systematic attempts to jam the radio. But despite ear-splitting noises, the message of the 'Voice' got through. The French then adopted further measures, and prohibited the sale of radios to Algerians, except with official permission. The possession of a radio in the urban area, or a school exercise book in a village, constituted enough evidence that the owners were F L N sympathizers. Such was the defeat of the French in the battle of ideas, that after 1957 the troops formed a habit of confiscating all radios in the course of a raid. They were regarded in the same light as illegal arms. The French also prohibited listening to certain broadcasts. The French colonizers had turned the radio into an instrument for the enslavement of the Algerian people. But with the launching of armed struggle by the F L N, the people of Algeria adopted the radio and fashioned it into a tool for moulding the Algerians into a nation.

The same could also be said about the French language.

There was initial resistance on the part of Algerians to the use of the French language. The nationalist organizations used Arabic in their rallies as well as their Congresses. Fanon explains that this was one of the ways to develop political consciousness by showing the difference between the oppressor and the oppressed : 'The Arabic language was the most effective means that the *nation's* being had of unveiling itself.'[5]

At the historic Soumman Conference in August 1956, the delegates used French and not Arabic : 'The fact that the discussions were carried on in French suddenly revealed to the occupation forces that the traditional general reticence of the Algerian with regard to using French within the colonial situation might no longer exist, when a decisive confrontation brought the will to national independence of the people and the dominant power face to face.'[6]

The use of French by those engaged in the revolution showed that they were beginning to be sure of themselves. At the stage when the rulers use their language as a means of cultural oppression, it is necessary to bring to the fore the people's language. But at every stage the revolution has to pause and examine its instruments, for it is crucial to determine what are the best methods and instruments to bring about the desired goal. If languages unite, they can also divide a people, for the proliferation of people's languages means that many of the people cannot understand each other. They sometimes guard their languages and are suspicious of other languages. The rulers use languages as one of their instruments to divide the people and to foster tribalism and clannishness.

Th 'Voice' soon began to broadcast in French as well as in Arabic. The French language of the 'Voice of Free Algeria' then became the language of revolution. At the same time, the F L N drove home a very important political message when its fidayeen exploded a number of time bombs on 'Radio Alger' with a view to silencing it. The lesson then was clear, that it was the *politics* which was conveyed through the French language which mattered, and not the employment of the French language.

The separation of the French language from French imperialism shows the political maturity of the leadership of the F L N. The Algerian people had nothing against the French language as such. The Revolution was against French imperialism and not the French people or their language. The French language was looked upon by the F L N as a tool to be used to further the interests of the revolution.

The experience of the Algerian revolution in the use of the French language has certainly had an impact on liberation movements in southern Africa which have taken the road of armed struggle. In Mozambique, Frelimo does not make a fetish of language. Since there is no common language spoken by the people which can be understood by all, Frelimo has decided to use Portuguese as the language to promote the revolution. In Angola, there are eight linguistic groups, and it was not possible to communicate in all the languages. The liberation movement, the M P L A, was faced with a choice. But to choose one of the people's languages would have created grave political problems. The result was that it decided on Portuguese. This did not mean that the other languages would be ignored, but that Portuguese would be the national language and be the medium of instruction in schools in liberated areas.

This then is a recognition by the revolutionaries that the question of language should be separated from oppression. Like the gun, it is a question of who wields it, and for what purpose? The Portuguese language could be used as a weapon to mould the new generation of Angolans and Mozambicans into understanding oppression and exploitation, exposing imperialism and neocolonialism, and recognizing the advantages of a co-operative way of life. The Portuguese language, therefore, is being used to win the battle of the mind, and is an essential instrument for winning the battle for liberation.

Fanon pointed out the irony of the situation when he

said that it was the struggle against French imperialism that helped to promote the French language. Before the revolution, French was spoken by only a small section of educated Algerians, and those who went to work in France. The Algerian revolution, using it as one of the means of communication, reached vast layers of people who had hitherto ignored the language. The French language was given a fillip by the same forces which were destroying French imperialism. It was the Algerian revolution which gave the French language its depth and scope in that country.

The same could also be said in Mozambique and Angola. Hitherto, Portuguese was restricted to urban areas only. In Angola, only about 15 per cent of the population is urbanized. The use of Portuguese in the liberated areas in the countryside means the spread of this language. So just as the Algerian revolution spread French, so too the Mozambican and Angolan revolutions are now spreading and popularizing the Portuguese language among the people, a thing which the colonialists failed to do.

Fanon, with his knowledge of psychiatry, is at his best in analysing the effects of all aspects of the liberation struggle on the minds of both the colonizer and the colonized. He is on less sure ground when dealing with problems of a purely political character. An example is the way in which he interpreted the attitude of the Communist Parties of France and of Algeria towards the Algerian revolution. In a series of articles in *El Moudjahid* in December 1957, Fanon noted that the French Communist Party was against the struggle for the independence of Algeria, and joined its own bourgeoisie in suppressing it. When the revolution broke out, the Communist Party of France branded the F L N as a band of terrorists, and gave full support to the French government to take drastic measures to defeat it. What this support meant in fact, was that French workers were called upon to kill their fellow Algerian workers.

The Communist Party of Algeria (C P A) followed the line of the French Communist Party. The C P A said that its dispute with the FLN was not only tactical, but programmatic. The CPA asserted that the people of Algeria must wait for the working class to triumph in France first. In other words, the Algerian liberation struggle was to be tied to the chariot wheels of the French Communist Party. The second argument advanced was that the CPA was not prepared to support a national movement which would replace the French bourgeoisie with an Algerian bourgeoisie. The practical effect of the stand taken by the CPA was to cut off from the national stream of struggle a section of the working class controlled by it. It was for this reason that the FLN decided to launch its own trade union movement which would be committed to supporting the revolution.

Fanon, in dealing with this attitude, wrote: 'We know that even the Algerian Communist Party was for a long time confined within a reformist position of the French Union type, and that for many months after 1 November 1954, the Algerian Communists denounced the *terroristes provocateurs* – in other words, the FLN.'[7] He gave a slightly different variation of the Communist Party rationalization of its position when he wrote: 'The French Communist Party, it says, can only support certain national liberation movements, for what would be the advantage of us French Communists, of having American imperialism take over Algeria?'[8]

The stand of the Communist Party of France had a damaging effect in the struggle to win the minds of intellectuals from the colonies. The ideologists of the bourgeoisie pressed home the point that the Communists appeared not to be interested in advancing the cause of oppressed peoples. The disillusionment and anger was expressed by men like Aimé Césaire when he declared that Marxism and Communism should serve the black people, and not the other way round.

The apparent treachery of the Communist Party to the cause of proletarian internationalism had a devastating effect on Fanon. Not only was he disillusioned about the Communist Party but also about communism. So disorientated did he become that he swallowed what the bourgeois ideologists were saying about the workers. He wrote : 'In a colonial country, it used to be said, there is a community of interests between the colonized people and the working class of the colonialist country. The history of the wars of liberation waged by the colonized peoples is the history of the non-verification of this thesis.'[9]

There is little doubt that today, Fanon would most likely have cast aside, or have modified this view. In the forefront of supporting liberation movements in central and southern Africa, in Guinea Bissau, in Palestine, in Indo-China and elsewhere, have been the workers and peasants of socialist countries. In some cases, support from socialist countries has even had the effect of goading some of the working-class parties of capitalist countries also to support liberation movements.

Fanon was swept away, and made this bald generalization because of his weak ideological anchor. He was not able to distinguish between a temporary phenomenon and a permanent one. From his limited experience of the role of the Communist Party of France and other reformist communist parties in Europe, he made a sweeping condemnation of the working class in a whole historical epoch. He failed to distinguish between the party of the working class which was following the political line of the proletariat, and the one which had the support of workers, but where the leadership's political line tended towards the bourgeoisie.

CONCLUSION

Comrades, we must turn over a new leaf, we must work out new concepts, and try to set afoot a new man.[1]

FANON did not live to see the end of the Algerian revolutionary war in 1962. He was already very ill when he returned from his travels throughout West Africa in 1960, and he went for urgent medical treatment in the Soviet Union. It seems that he did not know then that he had leukaemia. According to an article written by Fanon's brother Joby, and published in *Le Monde* on 3 March 1969, Frantz thought he was suffering from anaemia. He only learnt that his illness was leukaemia when he returned to Tunisia from the Soviet Union early in 1961. Joby said that the illness was diagnosed by Fanon's friend and colleague Dr Juminer. But with characteristic courage and determination Fanon continued his political work and taxed his failing health even further by working on the final part of *The Wretched of the Earth.*

In August, Fanon met Sartre in Rome and asked him to write a Preface for the book. But by the end of September 1961, Fanon's condition had deteriorated so badly that he agreed to seek further treatment in the USA. In an article written by Joseph Alsop, published in the *Washington Post* on 21 February 1969, it was claimed that Fanon had asked CIA representatives in Algeria for medical help after he returned from the USSR in February 1961. Apparently, Fanon had been told that he could get the best treatment for his particular condition in the USA. Alsop claimed that a CIA agent accompanied Fanon to the USA and arranged for his hospitalization. As in the case of the premature deaths of so many revolutionaries speculation remains on the role of reactionary intelligence organizations on Fanon's death. First, it is not clear why Fanon, if so seriously ill, remained for a full week in a hotel in Washington before being admitted to hospital. He stayed in the Dupont Plaza Hotel from 3-10 October before being admitted to the National Health Institute, Bethseda. He died there on 6 December, just after the publication in Paris of *The Wretched of the Earth*. He was only thirty six.

Secondly, while Alsop asserted that Fanon's only visitors at the hospital were his wife and six year old son, Joby Fanon has said that his brother was visited by many friends, among them Alioune Diop of *Présence Africaine*, and Roberto Holden of Angola. In addition, Joby asserts that arrangements for Fanon's hospitalization were made by the Algerian Mission to Washington and the Department of State. Thirdly, the cause of Fanon's death was given as 'double bronchial pneumonia', and not as one might have expected 'leukaemia'.

One month before he died, Fanon wrote to his friend Roger Tayeb:

Translation
> Roger I want to tell you that death is always with us and the question is not whether we can escape it, but whether we have achieved the utmost for our ideals. As I lie here, my strength ebbing as the blood weakens, what strikes me is not the fact of death – I could have died three months ago in action against the enemy when I knew that I was already doomed by this sickness. No, we are nothing if we are not from the beginning devoted to a cause, the cause of the people, the cause of justice and liberty. I'd like you to know that even when the doctors pronounced sentence on me I was thinking through the mists around me of the Algerian people, of the people of the third world and of you. For if I have been able to withstand the blow it is thanks to you.

Fanon's body was flown back to Tunisia, and on the request of the F L N he was buried, appropriately in a cemetery of the A L N on Algerian soil. Speaking at the funeral, Belkacem Krim, Vice-President of the G P R A, referred to Fanon's immense contribution to the Algerian revolutionary struggle and to the African Revolution as a whole. He ended:

Frantz Fanon! Your example will live for ever. Rest in peace. Algeria will not forget you.

Fanon was head and shoulders above most of his contemporaries in the clarity of his vision and literary powers, and he gave all he had to the Algerian Revolution. It is small wonder that the revolutionary nationalists claim him as one of them, even though he came from an island thousands of miles away.

He possessed a quality found in great men throughout the ages, intellectual honesty and courage. He refused to be silenced when principles were being violated, or when man's dignity and honour were being sacrificed. He gave up a steady, well-paid job which promised him personal security for the rest of his life, for the dangers and uncertainties of the life of a revolutionary. Although he did not occupy any important position in the leadership in the F L N, he was a hunted man. Several attempts were made to assassinate or to capture him. Thus he too had to face the same dangers as any militant or cadre of the F L N.

He packed a lot of experience into his short life. He was a soldier under De Gaulle, a medical student at Lyons University, an author in Paris, a doctor in Algeria, a journalist and freedom fighter in Tunisia, a secret agent and explorer in Mali, and an ambassador in Ghana. Though he felt at ease with western intellectuals and with diplomats, he was equally at home with the *fellahs* in Algeria, or with the workers of the Casbah. Fanon was part of the western intellectual world which was producing then the world's leading dramatists, philosophers, poets and novelists. Being a doctor, and an author, he was accepted as one of them. He gave these circles his views on art and medicine. He made them aware of the Algerian and colonial revolution.

The colonial bourgeoisie gave education to a strata of the oppressed and thereby cut them off from the masses. With Fanon the result was just the opposite. He joined the masses and brought with him his education, knowledge, skills and contacts which would be useful to the revolution. In this respect he was very much like Eduardo Mondlane, founder of Frelimo, and Amilcar Cabral, founder of P A I G C who, after acquiring the best education that capitalism could offer, placed it at the disposal of the liberation movements.

Whatever Fanon did it was with zeal, sincerity and devotion. Unlike the intellectuals of his generation he was not cynical. He was an optimist and remained one throughout his life. As editor of the student magazine *Tom Tom* he was zealous and enthusiastic. As a doctor in Blida Hospital he was conscientious, humane and sympathetic. As a freedom fighter and a journalist he was a crusader for a cause. Wherever he went, he inspired those around him by the sheer force of his personality, the strength of his commitment, and the high quality of his work. Some of the best issues of *El Moudjahid* appeared when he was on its editorial board. Implicit in his attitude to life was his belief that whatever one gives, whether in the realm of ideas or in practical effort, it must be of the best.

In one sense, Fanon was a lonely man. In fact, this is the condition of most revolutionaries who are ahead of their contemporaries. But it particularly pained Fanon to find that many of his fellow African intellectuals were not able to shed all their prejudices and superstitions despite their education. Centuries of oppression had left its mark on them, robbing them of confidence in themselves. Such intellectuals tended to regard the white man either as a superior, or as one who could not be trusted whatever his political views. It was this reverse racialism which Fanon could not stomach, because it was completely alien to his thought. While he was a determined foe of French imperialism, he made a distinction between it and the French people. In his writings, more often than not, he addressed himself to the French people, particularly to the French intellectuals to commit themselves to the side of the Algerian revolution. It saddened him to meet African intellectuals who were prepared to accept him, and not his wife. Their distrust of Josie was because she was white, and because she was French.

There is little doubt that the Algerian revolution has had a great impact on the liberation movements in other parts of Africa. Fanon is widely read, and his record of the struggles of the F L N is carefully studied. Party militants have found Fanon's advice sound in that they have not waited for the 'objective conditions to mature', the advice of the French Communist Party, but have gone ahead like the F L N did, after a period of political work in the countryside. They have not waited for the formation of vanguard parties. The party militants of the armed forces have acted as the vanguard. Political consciousness grows in the process of struggle, and the leaders of Frelimo, P A I G C, M P L A, and S W A P O, to name a few of Africa's liberation movements, have stated the necessity of having politically-conscious cadres in the national front. If these leaders are posing some of the issues more sharply than Fanon did, it is because they want to avoid some of the mistakes made in Algeria.

The present freedom fighters of Africa look upon Fanon as a comrade who courageously raised the banner of armed struggle at a time when the national liberation movement was infected with Gandhism. It required courage and foresight to say that the national bourgeoisie was bankrupt and utterly incapable of leading society forward. Yet Fanon fearlessly exposed this class as parasitic and self-seeking. These same freedom fighters also remember Fanon for his warnings about tribalism and racism, and the dangers of compromise. He showed how the reformist leadership of national movements is prepared to barter away the rights of peasants and workers in return for flag independence.

Fanon has been criticized, and correctly so, for his sweeping generalizations, his inconsistencies and his obvious exaggerations. He has been charged, and again with justice, for relying on superficial impressions and for his lack of historical method in analysing problems. Yet in his writings he expressed thoughts which will not be dimmed with the passage of time. Generations of workers, peasants and intellectuals, bent on completing the unfinished revolution will turn to Fanon repeatedly. Likewise, the national liberation movements in central and southern Africa and Guinea Bissau will be grateful to him, for he helped them to climb the first few steps of the ladder. He was able to feel the pulse of the African Revolution. Fanon wrote passionately and colourfully. In this he was reflecting the Revolution's many-sidedness and its complexities.

In the very process of growth, many of Africa's contemporary revolutionaries are now leaving Fanon behind for they are grappling with problems of a cadre party which must be armed with a clear ideology. They are facing class struggle within liberation movements; problems arising from the composition of the national front and its leadership; and the special difficulties and problems arising out of the administration of liberated areas. Fanon reflected the ferment that was taking place in Africa. But his thoughts had still to crystallize. If he adopted contradictory positions it was because he reflected the changes which were taking place around him, and which were in a process of flux.

Fanon did not advocate violence for its own sake. If he had done, he would have been a homicidal maniac and not a revolutionary. He advocated violence in order to bring about a total and authentic decolonization. He considered violence as the highest form of political struggle. The violence of the colonizer had to be met with the revolutionary violence of the colonized, so that not only would colonial rule be ended, but also the whole system of exploitation. For no exploiter voluntarily surrenders power. And, in the course of armed struggle, genuine advances can also be made in the political education of the masses. 'Violence alone, violence committed by the people, violence organized and educated by its leaders, makes it possible for the masses to understand social truths and gives the key to them. Without that struggle, without that knowledge of the practice of action, there's nothing but a fancy-dress parade and the blare of trumpets. There's nothing save a minimum of readaptation, a few reforms at the top, a flag waving : and down there at the bottom an undivided mass, still living in the Middle Ages, endlessly marking time.'[2]

Fanon in his writings mirrored a phase in the national movement which had its hopes and illusions. Its hopes were to create a better world. Its illusions consisted of some ideas which could never bring about the realization of these hopes.

The 'Third World' for which Fanon is regarded as a spokesman, is a world mainly of peasants. But the peasant alone cannot create a new world order. The peasant can fight, he can sacrifice, he can even overthrow a regime, but he cannot bring into being a new economic system. Either the peasant has to link his destiny with the proletariat, or he has to get tied up with the bourgeoisie. If the latter, it means further suffering and sacrifice, and he has to prepare for another revolution. If it is the former, then it will mean a new society where he will be the master of his own destiny.

Finally, while visiting Mali in 1960, Fanon jotted down a few thoughts on the possible unification of Africa. How could this great task be achieved? He was certain of one thing, that the bourgeoisie could never accomplish it. 'We must understand that African unity can only be achieved through the upward thrust of the people, and under the leadership of the people, that is to say, in defiance of the interests of the bourgeoisie.'[3] Kwame Nkrumah has declared the same thing, more concisely: 'The political unification of Africa and socialism are synonymous. One cannot be achieved without the other.'[4]

A further point on which Fanon shows great insight, and prophetic vision, is on the danger of the entry into politics of Africa's professional armies. In 1960, before the rash of military coups in Africa, Fanon wrote: 'Care must be taken to avoid turning the army into an autonomous body which sooner or later, finding itself idle and without any definite mission, will 'go into politics' and threaten the government. Drawing-room generals, by dint of haunting the corridors of government departments, come to dream of manifestoes. The only way to avoid this menace is to educate the army politically, in other words to nationalize it. In the same way another urgent task is to increase the militia.'[5] Again, Nkrumah, writing in Conakry some ten years later, after a succession of army coups had taken place in Africa, endorses Fanon's thesis: 'The rash of military coups in Africa reveals the lack of socialist revolutionary organization, the need for the founding of an all-African vanguard working class party, and for the creation of an all-African people's army and militia.'[6]

Kwame Nkrumah, the man whom Fanon if he were living today might have hailed as the much-needed ideologist of the African Revolution, had come to the conclusion that the total liberation and unification of the continent can only be accomplished by revolutionaries committed to scientific socialism. Fanon, although he had not accepted scientific socialism as such, had arrived at basically the same conclusion by the time he died.

APPENDIX

Proceedings of the Soumman Conference. Extracts from the Platform

[Translation]

To assure the triumph of the Algerian Revolution

The object of the present platform is to define in general the position of the FLN during the crucial period of the Algerian revolution.

It is divided into three parts:

1. The present situation
2. General perspective
3. Means of action and propaganda

For the last ten years Algeria has been fighting heroically for national independence. The patriotic and anticolonial revolution is marching forward. It is winning world-wide admiration. In a relatively short period the FLN army concentrated in Aures and Kabyles has achieved tremendous success. It has succeeded in spite of the campaign of encirclement and annihilation led by strong and modern military forces of a colonial regime representing one of the great powers of the world. Despite its temporary lack of arms it has developed guerrilla and sabotage operations engulfing the whole territory. It has constantly consolidated its position by improving its tactics, techniques and skills. It has passed rapidly from guerrilla warfare to partial total war. It has combined the approved methods of anticolonial war with more classical methods and has adapted them to the country's situation. It has already furnished sufficient proof that its military organization is unified and that it possesses a scientific strategy of war covering the whole of Algeria.

The National Liberation Army is fighting a just war. It groups together patriots, volunteers and fighters who have decided to continue the struggle until the motherland is freed. It is reinforced by patriotic officers, sub-officers and soldiers of the supply and combat contingents who have deserted *en masse* from the French army with their arms and supplies.

For the first time in military annals, France can no longer rely on the 'loyalty' of Algerian troops. Thus they are obliged to transfer them to France or Germany. The native mounted soldiers (harkas), recruited from among the unemployed, having been cheated as to the nature of the 'work' for which they have been enlisted are often demoralized. Many of them are disarmed and disbanded by the equally demoralized authority.

The human reserves of the ALN are inexhaustible. The army is often forced to refuse the enrolment of young and old Algerians from towns and countryside who earnestly seek the honour of joining their army. The army fully enjoys the love of the Algerian people, their enthusiastic support, their active, total and indestructible solidarity both moral and material. Senior officers, zone commanders, political commissars, cadres and soldiers of the ALN are honoured as national heroes. They are glorified in popular songs which have already penetrated humble shacks and tents as well as houses and villas. The essence of the 'Algerian miracle' is that the ALN is defeating the colossal forces of the French colonialists, reinforced by units of NATO. This is why, despite the non-stop reinforcement which has proved insufficient, despite new techniques and tactics, despite the heaviest bombardments, the French generals are obliged to recognize that a military solution cannot be found for resolving the Algerian problem.

We must draw attention to the formation of several urban guerrilla groups which already constitute a second army without uniform. Armed groups in towns and villages have distinguished themselves by attacks upon police stations and gendarme posts. They have sabotaged public buildings, set enemy installations alight, and have eliminated many police officers, informers and traitors. This weakens considerably the military and police strength of the colonialist enemy and increases the desperation of their forces on the national soil. It also increases the deterioration of the morale of the troops who are constantly kept in a state of nervousness and exhaustion caused by the necessity of being alert all the time.

It is an undeniable fact that the actions of the ALN have completely changed the political climate in Algeria. They have provoked a psychological shock which has liberated the people from their torpor, their fear, and from their scepticism. It has made the Algerian people conscious of their national dignity. It has also caused a movement towards the political unity of all Algerians, a national unanimity which fertilizes the armed struggle and renders inevitable the final victory of the fight for freedom.

An effective political organization
In spite of its clandestine actions the National Liberation Front has today become a unique and real national organization. Its influence cannot be denied throughout the territory. In fact, within a very short period, the FLN has succeeded in bringing about the end of all the political parties which existed during the past several decades. This was not haphazard. It resulted from the following:

1. The abolition of personal power and the substitution of the principle of a collective leadership of people who are honest and courageous and who do not fear any danger, prison or death.
2. Absolute clarity of doctrine. The aim is to achieve national independence. The means to achieve it is a revolution by destroying the colonial regime.
3. The union of the people is realized through struggling against the common enemy without sectarianism.

The FLN affirmed at the beginning of the revolution that 'the liberation of Algeria will be a task of all Algerians and not of a fraction of her people whatever its importance.' That is why the FLN takes into consideration within its struggle all anti-colonialist forces, even if they still are outside its control.

There is open struggle against adventurists, informers, stooges, spies and police officers.

As a result of these policies, the FLN has been able to escape all the political manoeuvres and traps laid by French police. However, this does not mean that all difficulties are completely eliminated. Our political actions have from the outset been handicapped for the following reasons:

- the numerical insufficiency of cadres and supplies, monetary and material
- the necessity for a long and hard struggle for political clarification, for patient and persevering explanation in order to overcome a grave and increasing crisis
- the strategic imperative of subordinating everything to the front of the armed struggle

These weaknesses, normal and inevitable at the beginning, have already been overcome. After a period when the FLN confined itself only to giving orders to resist imperialism, one can now see how the FLN is entering fully into the field of political struggle. This change was marked by the strike on the day of the first anniversary of 1st November 1956. It was considered as a decisive event as much for its spectacular and positive aspect as for its profound nature which proved the importance of winning the hearts of all layers of the population. Never in the memory of Algerians has any political organization been able to organize such a large scale strike in the towns and villages of the country.

On the other hand, the campaign of political non-co-operation launched by the FLN is no less convincing. The succession of resignations of patriotic representatives in government service has forced the French government not to renew the mandate of the members of the Bourbon Palace, and has caused the dissolution of the Algerian Parliament. The general and municipal councils and the *djemaas* have disappeared. This emptiness became accentuated and amplified by the resignation of numerous functionaries and auxiliaries of the colonial authority, *caids*, divisional chiefs and village policemen. Faced with lack of candidates or of replacements, the French administration is thus in disarray. Its workforce, considered as insufficient, does not get any support from among the people; in almost all regions it coexists with the authority of the FLN. This slow but profound disintegration of the French administration has permitted the birth and then the development of a duality of power. A revolutionary administration already functions side by side with clandestine *djemaas*. These organizations deal with logistics, taxation, justice, recruitment of freedom fighters, security and information services.

The FLN administration will present a new appearance with the institution of peoples' assemblies which will be elected by the rural population before the second anniversary of our revolution.

The political orientation of the FLN is strongly confirmed by its massive peasant support. For the winning of national independence signifies at the same time agrarian reform which will assure peasants the possession of the land they make fertile with their labour. This aspect of our struggle has been manifested by an upsurge of insurrectional activity which has spread rapidly throughout the country in many and varied ways.

The presence of elements of townspeople, politically aware and experienced under the clear leadership of the FLN has facilitated the politicization of the backward regions. The support of students has been very useful, mainly in the domains of politics, administration and health.

What is certain is that the Algerian revolution has just passed with honour the first historic period. It is a living reality, having triumphed despite the French colonialist threat to destroy it within four months. It is an organized revolution and not an anarchist revolt. It is a national struggle to destroy the anarchist regime of colonization, and is not a religious war. It is a step forward in the history of humanity and not a return to feudalism. And it is a struggle for the birth of an Algerian state in the form of a democratic and social republic, and is not a restoration of a monarchy or a dead theocracy.

Bankruptcy of old political formations
The Algerian revolution has accelerated the political maturity of the Algerian people. It has shown them in the course of the liberation struggle the weakness of reformism and the sterility of counter-revolutionary charlatanism. The bankruptcy of the old parties has come out into the open and various groups have been abandoned. Grassroots militants have joined the FLN, UDMA and the Ulemas and have courageously aligned themselves with the FLN. UDMA, which combines all university and high school students, has also expressed the same sentiments through unanimous support at their congress. The Central Committee of MTLD has completely disappeared as a group of ex-leaders and as a political trend. The MNA despite demagogy and outbidding has not succeeded in surmounting the mortal crisis of the MTLD. It maintains a foothold only in France due to the presence of Messali in exile, and due to the immigrants' ignorance of the realities in Algeria. It is from there that the funds and the people come who form in Algeria armed troops or dissident guerrillas destined not to join the struggle against the enemy, the army and police of the colonial regime, but to sabotage and deprive the Algerian revolution of its military and political leaders.

The brief and sporadic activity of the MNA had shown itself in towns such as Algiers in the form of a counter-revolutionary sect indulging in operations of diversion and gangsterism, of confusion and lies, Messali being the self-styled creator and chief of the national liberation army. 'Messalism' has lost credibility in the present political situation. It has become more and more a state of mind which daily deteriorates.

It is specially significant that the last admirers and defenders of Messali should be precisely the journalists and intellectuals close to the President of France. They pretend to denounce the ingratitude of Algerians who do not recognize any more the 'exceptional merit' of Messali who thirty years ago created

Algerian nationalism. The psychology of Messali resembles that of the legendary cock who, not satisfied with heralding the dawn, claims to cause the sun to rise.

Algerian nationalism which Messali claims to have founded is a universal phenomenon, a result of natural evolution followed by all peoples emerging from their lethargy. The sun rises irrespective of the cock. So the Algerian revolution succeeds regardless of Messali. The praise of 'Messalism' in the French press is a serious indication of a psychological preparation for a big offensive against the Algerian revolution. It is a typical colonialist tactic of divide and rule.

. . . .

The Resident Minister, Lacoste, did not hesitate to confide in the colonialist press his satisfaction at seeing the MNA making unique efforts to weaken the FLN. A socialist daily, *Demain*, revealing tactical differences dividing the French rulers, could write that certain ministers had arranged to give total freedom to Messali in order to stop the reinforcement of the FLN. But the problem as they see it is to ensure the safety of the Algerian leaders. When one remembers that Messali indulged in a strong attack against the Arab countries which can only please the enemy, then his replacement justifies the theme of *Demain*. When the life of Messali is so precious for French colonialism can one be surprised to see him slipping into a conscious treason?

Absent communism

The PCA despite its passage into illegality and the noisy publicity accorded to it by the colonialist press in order to justify an imaginary clash has not succeeded in playing a role worth talking about. The communist bureaucratic leadership, without any contact with the people has not been capable of analysing the situation correctly. That is why it has condemned 'terrorism' and since the first month of the insurrection ordered the militants from Aures, who came to Algeria to seek guidance, not to take up arms. The PCA has disappeared as a serious organization above all because of the preponderance inside it of European elements whose nationalism has come out into the open in face of armed resistance. This lack of homogeneity and a coherent political line is a result of confusion and a belief in the impossibility of the national liberation of Algeria before the triumph of a proletarian revolution in France. This ideology which avoids reality is reminiscent of the concept of SFIO. It favours the politics of passive assimilation and of opportunism. Denying the revolutionary character of the peasantry and of the Algerian *fellahs* in particular, they pretend to be defending the Algerian working class against the possible danger of falling under the domination of the Arab bourgeoisie, as if Algerian national independence has necessarily to follow the path of previous abortive revolutions, or even march backwards towards some kind of feudalism. The CGT (General Confederation of Workers), under communist influence, finds itself in a similar situation, without being able to announce or to apply any action.

The general passivity of workers' movements, aggravated to some extent by the unfortunate attitude of FO and CFTC, is not due to the workers' lack of militancy but is a result of apathy among cadres of UGSA, who accept with folded arms orders from Paris. Many workers have understood that this day of patriotic action should have revived a character of national unanimity, clearly demonstrative, more dynamic, more profound, if workers' movements had been intelligently trained in a general struggle by a real central national trade union. This true assessment is shown to be entirely confirmed in the complete success of the patriotic strike of 5th July 1956. This is why Algerian workers have welcomed the birth of UGTA whose constant development is irresistible, as an expression of their impatient desire to take an active part in the smashing of colonialism which is at the root of misery, unemployment, emigration and human indignity.

.   .   .   .

Meanwhile one can observe certain individual communists making efforts to infiltrate into the ranks of the FLN and ALN. It is possible that this shows individual unrest and a desire to return to the sanity of national liberation. It is certain that in future the PCA will exploit this opportunity to hide its total isolation from the historic struggle of the Algerian revolution.

French imperialist strategy
The Algerian revolution destroying all colonialist forecasts continues to develop with exceptional vigour. It uproots and destroys the remains of the declining French empire. Successive governments are subjected to unprecedented political crises. Forced to pull out of Asian colonies they believe it possible to preserve those in Africa. Being unable to stop the 'rotting' of North Africa, they have descended on Tunisia and Morocco in order to guard Algeria.

Lessons from the Tunisian and Moroccan experiences
This policy has resulted in a succession of moral defeats in all sectors; workers' strikes, discontent in France, agitation among the peasants, budget deficits, inflation, under-production, economic bankruptcy, the Algerian question at the UN, etc.

The revolutionary push in North Africa, despite the absence of a common political strategy due to the organic weakness of the erstwhile committee of Magreb liberation, has forced the French colonialists to mount a quick defensive tactic and to scrap all traditionally repressive plans.

The sudden change in the colonialists' methods when they stopped being immobile in order to engage themselves in a search for an immediate solution was dictated basically by reasons of a strategic nature:

1. To stop the formation of a second front preventing the unification of armed struggle in Riff and Algeria.
2. To crush the unity of combat in three countries in North Africa.
3. To isolate the Algerian Revolution whose popularity renders it dangerous.

All these attempts were bound to fail. The negotiations made separately were aimed at duping or corrupting certain leaders in the sister states and pushing them into abandoning consciously or otherwise the battlefield of revolutionary struggle. The political situation in North Africa is characterized by the fact that the Algerian problem is inseparable from that of Morocco and of Tunisia. In fact, without the independence of Algeria, the freedom of Morocco and Tunisia is jeopardized. Moroccans and Tunisians have not forgotten that the conquest of their countries was made after the conquest of Algeria. The peoples of the Magreb are today convinced by experience that fighting isolated battles against a common enemy can only result in defeat for all. It is an error of judgement to think that Morocco and Tunisia can achieve real independence when Algeria still remains under the colonial yoke.

Colonialist rulers who are expert in diplomatic hypocrisy and who can take with one hand what they give with the other, will always dream of reconquering these countries whenever the international situation seems favourable. On the other hand, it is important to note that Moroccan and Tunisian leaders in their recent declarations adopt a viewpoint in support of the FLN.

A political solution was at first only considered by two schools of thought; those who advocated consulting Algerians through free elections, and those who advocated a cease-fire. Fragmentary reforms were proclaimed amidst general indifference: initially no parliamentary representation at Bourbon Palace, the dissolution of the Algerian Assembly, a timid purge of the police, the replacing of the 'three' senior officials, the increasing of agricultural wages, the access of Moslems to positions of public leadership, agrarian reform, election to the sole college. Today, Guy Mollet announces the existence of six or seven status projects for Algeria. There would be two assemblies – the first legislative and the second economic with a government composed of ministers or commissioners and presided over by a minister of the French government. This demonstrates on the one side an evolution, due to our struggle, of public opinion in France and on the other hand the mad dream of the French government that we would accept a false compromise of this sort.

. . . .

The FLN will, as in the past, frustrate the enemy's plans.

Political perspectives
It has been proved that the Algerian revolution is not an anarchist revolt, which is limited, without coordination, without political direction, and which is bound to fail. On the contrary, it is a genuine organized revolution, national and popular, centralized under a leadership capable of leading it to final victory.

It is a fact that the French government, having been convinced of the impossibility of a military solution is forced to search for a political solution. This is why the FLN has thoroughly to understand the principle that a negotiation follows a bitter struggle against a ruthless enemy; it never precedes it. Our position in this regard is the result of adhering to three essential principles and courses of action:

1. To have a clear political doctrine
2. To develop a continuous armed struggle until a general insurrection is accomplished
3. To engage in political action on a grand scale.

Why are we fighting
The Algerian revolution has a historic mission to destroy completely the decadent and obnoxious colonial regime which is an obstacle to progress and peace.

Objectives

The aim of the war is to end the fighting when the objective of peace is achieved. The aim is to create a situation whereby the enemy is pushed into accepting peace. It can be a military victory, a cease fire, or even an armistice with a view to negotiation. It is clear that in view of our present situation our aims are politico-military. They are:

1. The total weakening of the French army in order to render it impossible for the French to win with arms.
2. To make the colonial economy deteriorate by sabotaging it and so rendering the normal administration of the country impossible.
3. The maximum disturbance of the situation in France in the economic and social field in order to render the continuation of the war impossible.
4. The isolating of France politically in the world.
5. To give the insurrection a character in conformity with international law, personalization of the army, recognizable political power, respect for military laws, the normal administration of liberated zones by the ALN.
6. To constantly support the people in the face of policies of extermination adopted by Frenchmen.

Cease fire conditions

A. *Political*

  (i) Recognition of a united Algerian nation. This is to stop the colonialist fiction of a 'French Algeria'.
  (ii) Recognition of Algeria's independence and sovereignty in all domains including national defence and diplomatic representation.
  (iii) The release of all Algerians imprisoned, detained or exiled because of their patriotic activity, before and after the national insurrection of 1st November 1954.
  (iv) Recognition of the FLN as the only organization representing the Algerian people, and competent for all negotiations. The FLN is guardian of, and responsible for, the ceasefire in the name of the people of Algeria.

B. *Military:*

  (i) Conditions for a ceasefire having been fulfilled, the spokesman for Algeria will still remain the FLN. All questions of representation of the Algerian people will be

exclusively within the domain of the FLN. No machination on the part of the French government will be admitted.
(ii) Negotiations are to be conducted on the basis of independence (defence and foreign representation included).
(iii) Fixing the agenda:
- Limits of the Algerian territory, the present limits including the Algerian Sahara.
- French minority (on the basis of an option between Algerian citizenship and alien status, i.e. no dual nationality)
- French properties, those belonging to France and to French citizens
- Transference of the administration
- Forms of French assistance and co-operation in the economic, monetary, social and cultural fields, etc.
- Any other points.

. . . .

North African Federation
A free and united Algeria, having crushed colonialism, will develop a new unity and brotherhood. But Algerians although they will never cease to strengthen the motherland will not degenerate into a nationalist chauvinism which is dogmatic and blind. This is why they are sincere North Africans attached passionately and clearly to the natural and necessary solidarity of the three Magreb countries. North Africa is by its geography, history, language, civilization and destiny a single unit. This solidarity must therefore be naturally translated into the creation of a Federation of the three North African states.

The three fraternal peoples have first of all an interest in organizing a common defence, common political philosophy and foreign policy, free monetary exchange, a common and rational plan of industrialization, a currency policy, education and the exchange of technical experts, cultural exchange, the joint exploration of mineral wealth in the Sahara regions.

The new tasks of the FLN
In the event of the opening of peace negotiations there should be no relaxation of vigilance or demobilization which might weaken the political cohesion of the people. On the contrary, the present stage of the Algerian revolution calls for a non-stop prosecution of the armed struggle, a consolidation of position, the development of the military and political forces of the resistance. The

opening of negotiations and the successful outcome are first of all dependent on the relationship of forces existing at present. This is why one should work ceaselessly to transform Algeria into a fertile and impregnable camp. This is the task which the FLN and ALN should fulfil with honour, and without delay.

In this objective our slogans remain as follows:

- All for the front of the armed struggle
- All for achieving a decisive victory

Algerian independence is no more a public demand, a dream which has for a long time eluded the Algerian people. Today it is an immediate goal which is to become a bright reality. The FLN is marching with giant strides towards victory in the military, political and diplomatic fields.

Our new objectives
To prepare at once and in a systematic manner a general insurrection, inseparable from national liberation:

- To weaken the military, police, administrative and political sectors of French colonialism
- To consider with great attention the technical side of the question, especially the handling of supplies
- To consolidate and improve the coordination of politico-military action
- To face up to the inevitable dividing tactics employed by the enemy, and to counter them through an intelligent and vigorous counter-offensive based on the development of the popular revolution for liberation
- To cement the national anti-imperialist union
- To rely on the social stratas which are the most numerous, the poorest, the most revolutionary, the *fellahs* and agricultural labourers
- To convince with patience and perseverance the retarding elements, to encourage the hesitant, the weak, the moderates and to awaken the politically-unaware
- To isolate the ultra-colonialists by making alliance with some liberal elements of European or Jewish origin even if their action is still timid or neutralist
- On an international scale to search to the maximum for material, moral and psychological support
- To increase the support of public opinion
- To develop diplomatic aid in gaining support for the Algerian cause from governments of countries neutralized

by France or insufficiently informed of the national character of the Algerian war

Means of action and propaganda

The general political perspectives already outlined shows ways in which the FLN will assure the complete victory of the noble war to free the motherland. We are going to state precisely our major policy lines on the Algerian, French and foreign levels: how to organize and lead millions of men in a gigantic battle. The psychological union of the Algerian people forged and consolidated in the armed struggle is today a historic reality. This patriotic and anticolonial national union constitutes the fundamental base of the principal political and military force of the resistance. It has to be maintained intact and dynamic and from time to time avoid inexcusable faults of sectarianism and opportunism which flow from the enemy's diabolical manoeuvres. The best way to do this is to maintain the FLN as the leading force of the Algerian revolution. This should not be taken to be the result of vanity or a spirit of self-sufficiency which is dangerous as well as despicable. It is an expression of a revolutionary principle. It is to realize a unity of command under a leadership which has already proved its capacity, its clear-sightedness and its loyalty to the cause of the Algerian people.

We should never forget that until the revolution is set in motion, the force of French imperialism will not only lie in its military and police power, but also in the weakness of the country which is dominated, divided and unprepared for an organized fight. Above all, French imperialism over a long period, benefits from the political insufficiency of leaders of diverse sectors of anticolonialist movements.

The existence of a powerful FLN, with roots deep down in all layers of the population, is indispensible. The FLN must:

- Organize cells throughout the country, in all towns, villages, localities, enterprises, firms, universities, colleges, etc.
- politicize the underground forces
- have political cadres who are experienced and who respect the structure of the organization. They must be vigilant and capable of taking the initiative
- reply with clarity and rapidity to all the lies and provocation of the enemy, to popularise the policies of the FLN through writing books, pamphlets, news-sheets etc. about all aspects of the struggle
- multiply centres of propaganda with the aid of typewriters,

newspapers, duplicators, the reproduction of national
documents of news bulletins or local tracts
- edit pamphlets on revolution and local bulletins containing
directives and advice to cadres
- grasp properly this principle: propaganda is not characterized by verbal violence, often sterile and without positive
content. At this time when the Algerian people are ripe for
positive and fruitful action, the language of the FLN must
reflect its maturity. It must be serious and dignified without
losing firmness, frankness and revolutionary force. Each
tract and interview involving the FLN is heard inter-
nationally. This is why we must show a real spirit of
responsibility which brings international prestige to an
Algeria which is marching towards liberty and independence.

 .   .   .   .

The FLN must be capable of channelling the immense waves
which arise from the patriotic enthusiasm of the nation. The
irresistible force of the popular rage should not disappear like the
extraordinary force of a storm which vanishes on the seashore.
To transform it into creative energy the FLN has undertaken a
colossal task involving millions of people.

It is necessary to organize all the complex branches of human
activity:

The peasantry

The massive participation of *fellahs* and farm labourers in the
revolution, the dominant proportion that it represents in the
national liberation army has profoundly marked the popular
character of Algerian resistance. To appreciate its exceptional
importance it suffices to examine the spectacular reversal of the
colonial agricultural policy. This policy was based essentially on
the theft of land, such expropriation continuing up to 1945-6.
The French government today favours agrarian reform. It does
not avoid the promise to distribute a part of irrigated land by
putting into effect the Martin law. But this remains a dead
letter after a personal veto of a high colonial officer. Lacoste
himself could dare to envisage, in this case, a revolutionary
measure, an expropriation of a part of the big estates. To maintain an equilibrium and to appease the furious opposition of the
big settlers, the French government had decided on the reform of
the *khammessat*. This is a deceptive measure which tends to make
people believe in the existence of an internal rivalry between

fellahs and *khammes*, when the tenant farmer system has naturally evolved towards a more equitable process, without official intervention, transforming itself into 'chourka benes' or an association by half. This change of tactic shows a profound confusion of colonialism in trying to cheat the peasantry in order to detach it from the revolution. This manoeuvre in the last analysis will not dupe the *fellahs* who have already defeated such old tricks of trying to separate artificially the Algerians into Berbers and hostile Arabs.

The peasant population is profoundly convinced that thirst for land will only be satisfied by the victory of national liberation. Real agrarian reform, a patriotic solution of rural misery, is inseparable from the total destruction of the colonial regime.

The FLN must concern itself deeply with this just, legitimate and social struggle.

.   .   .   .

Workers' movement
The working class must and can make a most dynamic contribution to the rapid evolution of the revolution to its full power and its final success. The FLN welcomes the creation of UGTA as an expression of a sensible reaction of the workers to the paralysing influence of the leaders of the CGT, FO and CFTC. UGTA is helping the wage-earning population to emerge from confusion and a wait-and-see policy.

The French socialist government and the neo-colonial leadership of FO are worrying about the international affiliation of UGTA to CISL whose aid to UGTA and to Moroccan central has been positive in the diverse national and external domains. The birth and development of UGTA has in fact provoked a profound universal interest. Its existence has immediately provoked a violent reaction. There has been commotion inside the CGT, abandoned *en masse* by the workers. Communist leaders have tried in vain to retain the most conscious cadres by trying to find in the ashes the spirit of the former CCTU whose slogan of Algerian independence was buried on the day of workers unity in 1935. But in order to become a national central head office it is not enough for the Paris affiliate of the CGT to modify its title, or to change its colour of card, or even to cut the umbilical cord.

.   .   .   .

UGTA is a reflection of the profound transformation which has occurred in the workers' movement at the end of a lay evolution, and above all after the revolutionary change provoked by the struggle for national independence. The new Algerian head office differs from other organizations like CGT, FO and CFTC in all domains notably by the absence of a tutelage, and by the rational structure, just orientation and the fraternal solidarity in Algeria in North Africa and throughout the world. The national character is shown not only in an organic independence destroying the inherent contradictions of a foreign tutelage, but also in a total liberty in defending the workers whose vital interests mingle with those of the entire nation. The leadership is formed not by elements emanating from an ethnic minority which has never suffered colonial oppression, which always tended to paternalize, but by patriots whose national conscience increases their struggle against the double oppression of social and racial hatred.

The 'vertebral column' does not consist of an aristocracy of workers but of the most numerous and the most exploited workers, dockers, miners, agricultural labourers, the real outcasts who have up till now been ignored. The revolutionary wind cleanses the climate inside the trade unions not only in getting rid of the revolutionary colonialist spirit and national chauvinism which it engenders, but in creating the conditions for a proletarian brotherhood, free from racialism.

Trade union activities
For a long time confined to economic and social demands and isolated from a general perspective these have become not a stumbling block to the anticolonial struggle but an accelerator in the fight for freedom and social justice. The Algerian working class, so far judged as under-age and not meriting emancipation, is called upon not to occupy a subordinate position in the French social movement, but to cooperate with the North African and international workers' union. UGSA and CGT will find themselves inevitably forced to follow the example of similar organizations in Tunisia and Morocco and give in entirely to UGTA, the authentic and unique national organization combining all Algerian workers without distinction.

The FLN must not neglect the political role which it can play in helping to complete the independent action of UGTA to secure its consolidation and growth. FLN militants must be among the most devoted and most active, always respecting democratic rules according to the traditions inside the free working-class movement.

. . . .

Youth organization
Algeria's youth possess a natural quality of dynamism. Moreover, it is characterized by a rare fact. It represents nearly half of the total population due to an exceptional demographic development. Also, it possesses an original maturity, a precocious maturity. Due to the misery of colonial oppression, it has passed rapidly from infancy to adulthood. The period of adolescence is singularly reduced. The young people follow passionately, without fear of death, the revolutionary organization which can lead them to the conquest of their pure ideal of liberty. The Algerian revolution, the feats of the ALN and the underground activities of the FLN fire their imagination which is filled with the most noble patriotic sentiments.

. . . .

Forming action committees for patriotic intellectuals
1. Propaganda. Independence for Algeria
2. Contact with liberal Frenchmen
3. Subscriptions

The FLN will have to assign to students specialized tasks in the spheres where they can render the best service, i.e. in politics, administration, culture, health, economic sectors, etc.

Organizing medical services
1. Surgeons, doctors, pharmacists, hospital workers
2. Medical care, medicine and first aid
3. Rural nurses, treatment of the sick and convalescents

Traders and artisans
There is a vacuum caused by the absence of a real union for traders and artisans led by patriots to ensure the defence of the Algerian economy. UGTA will therefore take an important place beside the sister organization for workers. The FLN must help it to develop rapidly by creating the most favourable political conditions. It must:
   (i) fight against taxes
   (ii) boycott colonialist wholesale merchants who actively support imperialist war.

Women's movements
In this sphere immense possibilities exist which are continually developing. We salute with emotion and admiration the high revolutionary courage of young girls and women, wives and mothers, of all our sister crusaders who actively participate,

sometimes arms in hand, for the sacred liberation of the motherland.

All of us know that Algerian women have actively participated in the many insurrections against French occupation which have occurred in Algeria since 1830. The main explosions of 1864 in Onled Saidi Cheick of South Oran, of 1871 in Kabyle, of 1916 in Aures and Mascara region have shown the ardent patriotism, even the supreme sacrifice of Algerian women. We are today convinced that the present revolution will end inevitably with the winning of independence.

The recent example of a young Kabyle girl who refused a marriage proposal from a coward outside the battlefield, illustrates magnificently the sublime morale which animates Algerian women. It is therefore possible to organize an indomitable and efficient fighting force in this sector through:
- moral support to the combatants
- information, liaison, supply services and care of refugees
- help to families and children of fighters, prisoners and detainees

The search for alliances

To liberate their motherland which is in chains the Algerians depend on themselves. However, political action like military science teaches us not to neglect any factor, even if apparently less important, in order to ensure complete victory. This is why the FLN has successfully undertaken the mobilization of all national energy. It will not allow the colonialist enemy to gain support from ethnic minorities in Algeria, to embark on campaigns against us in France, and to isolate us from international support.

REFERENCES

Chapter One   From Martinique

1 Fanon, *Toward the African Revolution*, Penguin Books, 1970, p. 30.
2 Ibid., p. 29.
3 Ibid., p. 28.
4 Ibid., p. 32.
5 Ibid.
6 *African Revolution*, p. 33.
7 Ibid., p. 34.
8 Ibid., p. 35.

Chapter Two   Black Skin, White Masks

1 *Black Skin, White Masks*, Paladin edition, 1970, p. 161.
2 Ibid., p. 11.
3 Ibid., p. 12.
4 Ibid., p. 15.
5 Ibid., p. 29.
6 Ibid.
7 Ibid.
8 Ibid.
9 *Black Skin, White Masks*, p. 23.
10 Ibid.
11 Ibid., p. 19
12 Ibid., p. 72.
13 Ibid., p. 64
14 Ibid., p. 73
15 Ibid, p. 131.
16 Ibid.
17 Ibid., pp. 26–7.

Chapter Three   Evolué ideology and the French Left

1 Fanon, *The Wretched of the Earth*, Penguin Books, 1967, p. 187.
2 Kwame Nkrumah, *Class Struggle in Africa*, Panaf Books, p. 25.
3 Karl Marx, *The Eighteenth Brumaire of Louis Bonaparte*, in Fanon, *Black Skin, White Masks*, Paladin, p. 159.
4 Marx, *British Rule in India*, Selected Works, Progress Publishers, Moscow, 1969, Vol I, p. 493.
5 Jean-Paul Sartre, *Les Temps Modernes*, in *Existentialism versus Marxism*, edited by George Novack, Dell Publishing Co., New York, 1966, p. 157.
6 *Existentialism versus Marxism*, p. 148.

7 Marx, *The Eighteenth Brumaire of Louis Bonaparte*, in *Existentialism versus Marxism*, p. 156.
8 Simone de Beauvoir, Autobiography, Vol. III, in *Existentialism versus Marxism*, p. 28.
9 Sartre, In a notebook, quoted by Simone de Beauvoir, Autobiography, Vol. III, in *Existentialism versus Marxism*, p. 28.
10 Sartre, Eulogy of Merlaeu-Ponty, in *Existentialism versus Marxism*, pp. 30–1.

Chapter Four Psychiatry and politics

1 *Toward the African Revolution*, p. 63.
2 Ibid., p. 14.
3 Ibid., p. 23.
4 *African Revolution*, p. 25.
5 Ibid., p. 63.
6 *El Moudjahid*, No. 10, September 1957, in *African Revolution*, p. 77.
7 *African Revolution*, p. 62.
8 Ibid., p. 63.
9 Ibid.
10 Ibid., p. 64.
11 Ibid.
12 Ibid., p. 63.

Chapter Five Fanon and the FLN

1 Fanon, *The Wretched of the Earth*, Penguin Books, 1967, p. 74.
2 Ibid., p. 255.
3 *El Moudjahid*, Vol. 2, p. 52.
4 *The Wretched of the Earth*, p. 48.

Chapter Six Armed struggle and the Accra all-African Peoples Conference, 1958

1 Kwame Nkrumah, *Africa Must Unite*, Panaf edition, 1970, Introduction, p. xv.
2 *The Wretched of the Earth*, p. 72.
3 *Africa Must Unite*, p. 18.
4 *The Wretched of the Earth*, p. 118.
5 Ibid., p. 72.
6 Ibid., p. 73.
7 Ibid., p. 74.
8 Ibid., p. 69.
9 Irene L. Gendzier, *Frantz Fanon*, Wildwood House, 1973, p. 147.
10 *Challenge of the Congo*, Panaf Books, 1969, Introduction, p. xiv.
11 Ibid., p. xv.
12 Fanon, *Toward the African Revolution*, Pelican Books, 1970, p. 160.
13 Ibid., p. 165.
14 Ibid., p. 161.
15 Ibid., p. 163.
16 Ibid. p. 167
17 Ibid., p. 161.

18 Article 10. Resolutions adopted by the all-African People's Conference, December 5–13, 1958.
19 *Toward the African Revolution*, p. 166.

Chapter Seven   Fanon and the national bourgeoisie

1 *The Wretched of the Earth*, p. 133.
2 Ibid., p. 122.
3 Ibid., p. 133.
4 Kwame Nkrumah, *Class Struggle in Africa*, Panaf Books 1970, p. 10.
5 Ibid., p. 12.
6 *The Wretched of the Earth*, pp. 121–2.
7 *Class Struggle in Africa*, p. 33.
8 Ibid., p. 60
9 Ibid.
10 Ibid., p. 12.

Chapter Eight   Classes in the Algerian Revolution

1 Fanon, *The Wretched of the Earth*, p. 47.
2 Ibid., p. 39
3 Ibid., p. 89
4 Ibid., p. 87.
5 Ibid., p. 103.

Chapter Nine   Fanon on racism

1 *El Moudjahid*, No. 10, September 1957.
2 *Toward the African Revolution*, p. 91
3 Fanon, *A Dying Colonialism*, Pelican Books, 1970, p. 134.
4 Ibid.
5 Ibid., p. 136.
6 Ibid., p. 137
7 Ibid., pp. 136–7.
8 Ibid., pp. 137–8.
9 Ibid., p. 139.

Chapter Ten   The role of women

1 *A Dying Colonialism*, p. 52.
2 Ibid., p. 24.
3 Ibid., pp. 87–8.
4 Ibid., pp. 33–4.
5 Ibid., p. 43.
6 Ibid., p. 90.
7 Ibid., p. 97.
8 Ibid., pp. 51–2.
9 Ibid., p. 91.
10 *Le Monde*, 15 August 1965.

Chapter Eleven To 'put Africa in motion'
1 *Toward the African Revolution*, pp. 187–8.
2 Ibid., p. 190.
3 Ibid., p. 189.
4 Ibid., p. 207.
5 Kwame Nkrumah, *Challenge of the Congo*, Panaf Books 1966, Introduction, p. xvi.
6 *Revolutionary Theories*, Monthly Review, Vol. 21, No. 1, May 1969, pp. 30–1.
7 *Toward the African Revolution*, p. 191.

Chapter Twelve Fanon and the reformist political party
1 *The Wretched of the Earth*, p. 151.
2 Ibid., p. 46.
3 Ibid., p. 48.
4 Ibid., p. 46.
5 Ibid., p. 92.
6 Ibid., p. 48.
7 Ibid.
8 Ibid., pp. 98–9.
9 Ibid., p. 99.
10 Ibid., p. 100.
11 Ibid., p. 136.
12 Ibid., p. 137.
13 Ibid., p. 138.
14 Ibid., p. 146.

Chapter Thirteen Problems of leadership
1 Le Duan, *Role of the Vietnamese Working Class and tasks of the Trade-Unions at the Present Stage*, Foreign Languages Publishing Home, Hanoi, 1969 p. 25.
2 *The Wretched of the Earth*, p. 86.
3 Ibid., p. 47.
4 Le Duan, *Role of the Vietnamese Working Class*, p. 26.
5 Le Duan, *On the Socialist Revolution in Vietnam*, Vol 1, Foreign Languages Publishing House, Hanoi, 1967, p. 90.
6 *Frontier*, Calcutta, 24 June 1972.
7 *Frontier*, Calcutta, 1 July 1972.
8 Ho Chi Minh, *Selected Works*, Publishing House, Hanoi, 1960, p. 769. Quoted in Le Duan, *The Vietnamese Revolution*, Hanoi, 1970, pp. 29–30
9 Truong-Chinh, *Forward along the path charted by Karl Marx*, Foreign Languages Publishing Home, Hanoi, 1969, p. 41.
10 Le Duan, *The Vietnamese Revolution*, p. 31.
11 Eduardo Mondlane, *The Struggle for Mozambique*, Penguin African Library, 1969, p. 116.
12 Ibid.

Chapter Fourteen   The battle of the mind

1 *Toward the African Revolution*, p. 196.
2 *A Dying Colonialism*, p. 57.
3 Ibid., p. 68.
4 Ibid. p. 70.
5 Ibid., p. 75.
6 Ibid., p. 74.
7 Ibid., p. 130.
8 *Toward the African Revolution*, p. 69.
9 Ibid., p. 92.

Conclusion

1 *The Wretched of the Earth*, p. 255.
2 Ibid., p. 118.
3 Ibid., p. 132.
4 Kwame Nkrumah, *Class Struggle in Africa*, p. 84.
5 *The Wretched of the Earth*, p. 163.
6 *Class Struggle in Africa*, p. 54.

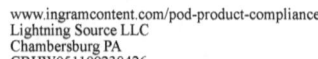

www.ingramcontent.com/pod-product-compliance
Lightning Source LLC
Chambersburg PA
CBHW051100230426
43667CB00013B/2374